MAMA BEAR

ONE MOM'S STORY OF OPTIMISM, AUTISM, ADVOCACY, AND LOVE

EL BROWN, M.ED.

Miche'!

Thank you for Changing lives!

xoxo

KinderJam Press Book
1934 Old Gallows Road, Suite 350
Tysons Corner, VA 22182
www.kinderjam.com

To protect the privacy of certain individuals some names and
identifying details have been changed. The events, locales and
conversations retold are based on the memories of the author.

Ordering Information:
Quantity sales. Special discounts are available on quantity
purchases by corporations, associations, and others. For
details, contact the publisher at the address above.
Orders by U.S. trade bookstores and wholesalers. Please
contact KinderJam, LLC: publishing@kinderjam.com

ISBN: 978-0-9909512-0-9

Printed in the United States of America

To all the parents who wake up every day and work tirelessly to create successful opportunities for their little ones. Your journey is my journey. Your tears are my tears. Your hopes are my hopes. Your triumphs are my triumphs. Our Super Kids need us, and together, We Got This!

April 5, 2011
A child doesn't know he isn't perfect until someone tells him so...
Plant seeds of positivity... Then shower with encouragement
and shine love all over them...and watch our children blossom
into their divine perfection... #mamabear

(8 weeks after SuperDuperKid's Diagnosis)

INTRODUCTION

NATURE VERSUS NURTURE is one of the oldest philosophical debates. Which affects a developing person more? Nature, the God-given genes and hereditary factors such as personality and physical appearances? Or is it Nurture, the environmental variables that impact a person's life, our early childhood experiences, how we were parented, the relationships we build, and the culture by which we are surrounded? Is it Nature or Nurture that determines personal greatness?

Or is it a combination of both?

If you were to argue on the side of Nurture, you would not be reading a book written by me, a child born to a teenager who was uninterested in being a mother. A child who didn't meet her father until the age of six. A child left to grow up unprotected and introduced to the evils of the world well before her young mind had an opportunity to develop a healthy defense. A child who moved twenty-eight times before her eighteenth birthday. A child who found herself homeless at eighteen and was taken in by the kindness of a friend. If Nurture was the factor that determined the development of a person, that child would have been doomed to a bleak and hopeless future.

However, it was the nature of that child's spirit that moved her from homelessness to a college dorm room. From a dorm room to a career as a teacher. From a teacher to living and working in Asia. From living and working in Asia to being a stay-at-home mom. And finally, from a stay-at-home mom to the founder and CEO of an international company with the mission of early childhood education, early intervention, and positive parent engagement. Look at God!

If you were to argue on the side of Nature, you would not be reading a book about the joyous and triumphant journey of my son, SuperDuperKid (SDK), who was born on the autism spectrum and has defied every odd to become a beacon of hope for families and a testament to the power of a strong support system and love without condition.

I believe great people are a perfect combination of the two.

I have had the heart of a lioness from as far back as I can remember, a fight in me that refused to let failure be an option. I didn't understand the purpose for that fight until I became the mother of my Super Duper Kid. Not until I was faced with having to have a voice for two.

In motherhood, the nature of the lion that had lived in me since childhood and the nurture of all the lessons, skills, and experience I had gained in young adulthood collided and formed my alter ego, Mama Bear.

Mama Bear is a champion and protector, and above all, completely and unconditionally in love with her cub.

Mama Bear is also an example that any person from any walk of life or any family background can learn the tools to effective and happy parenting. To break the cycle of dysfunctional childhood environments. To create every opportunity to maximize a child's personal potential. And to build a village that collectively celebrates, supports, and advocates for your child's place in this world. Your child needs, trusts, and is depending on you. Your child deserves for you to develop and unleash your inner Mama (or Papa) Bear.

From my Mama Bear to yours—We Got This!

PART I
MEET MAMA BEAR

FIRST GENERATION COLLEGE STUDENT

AFTER MY HIGH school graduation, I took a job in a local grocery store. One day a former classmate came through my line.

"Hi, Linda. I haven't seen you in a while. Where have you been?"

"Oh, I've been away at college. I go to Florida A&M University," she answered with an air of haughtiness.

I thought to myself, *Wait a minute! If she can go to college, I know I can.*

That conversation changed the course of my life.

I had recently been kicked out of my mother's home and had been living for some time with my belongings in the back of my 1978 Ford Fairmont. After a short stint of staying with a friend and her family, my grandparents invited me to live with them. One morning I overheard a conversation between my grandparents and realized my stay with them would be short-lived.

In my family, you are considered grown at eighteen. I graduated from high school at seventeen, which meant I already had more education than the majority of my family members. I was smart, and the expectation was for me to get a job and "be grown"… whatever that meant.

Although I was eighteen years old, I had never been actively parented or trained as a young lady, so I was a little lost. By God's grace, I was blessed with enough common sense to realize I did not yet have the tools to successfully navigate the world as an adult on my own. My short conversation with Lisa in my check-out line presented me with an option.

After overhearing my grandparents' conversation, I got up, got dressed, and drove to my old high school. I parked my car and took a deep breath before I walked to my former guidance counselor's office. Fortunately, he was available to see me. I could tell he was baffled by my visit, but I didn't know where else to go. Through my tears I spoke one of the bravest sentences I have even spoken in my life.

"I need to go to college because I need a place to stay."

I watched his face as he tried to process my words. I wondered if I had shared too much, but I kept going.

"I need your help."

He got up from his chair and reached for a book on his shelf. It was a yearbook from Florida A&M University, his Alma Mater. He sat down, placed the book in front of me, and said, "I went to FAMU. Would you like to go?"

I smiled and said that I would. Mr. Williams walked me through the steps of requesting my transcripts and gave me the application.

Afterward, I went to see a friend whose parents had attended Florida A&M University, and asked her father to help me fill out my college application. As I was completing the application, I began to feel very afraid. There were many blank spaces where extracurricular activities should have gone. I'd had a job since I was fourteen years old and had little time or support for much else. I decided to include a handwritten note with my application to explain that my grades and lack of activities did not represent the person that I was and if given the opportunity to attend their university, I would make them proud.

Florida A&M University accepted me and saved my life.

A few months later, I arrived at Florida A&M University in my 1978 Ford Fairmont (which promptly broke down on me as soon as I arrived in Tallahassee) with my clothes packed in banana boxes. I assumed every student would be arriving alone just like me. Imagine my surprise when I saw the leagues of minivans bringing their beloved children to college. I realized in that moment that the family unit was common and not an anomaly reserved for a few select privileged people.

Like an explorer, I began to study my friends and their family relationships, intrigued that many of my college classmates came from homes with loving parents who made it their life's work to create successful opportunities for their children. I decided this is what I wanted to give to my own child one day. I just needed a map to guide me.

The first thing I noticed about these families was that many of the mothers were teachers. I'd never had any real desire to become a teacher, but if that was the training ground for becoming a mother, then elementary education was where I needed to be. Although I would not meet my son for another eleven years, changing my major from political science to elementary education during my second semester was the first deliberate step I took in preparation to becoming a parent.

During my four years at FAMU, I was exposed to skills and

strategies that would prove invaluable in my role as my son's first educator. After graduation, I had an extremely rewarding career as a classroom teacher. I taught fourth and third grades, respectively, in the US, before journeying to Japan to teach second grade.

DISCOVERING THE INDIVIDUALITY OF CHILDREN

MY FIRST YEAR as a teacher for the Department of Defense Education Activity served as the next training ground for becoming my son's mother. Up until this point, I had viewed teaching as more of a profession than my calling. But while in Japan, my passion for teaching was ignited. Second grade is the perfect time to watch a child's personality blossom and have a hand in his or her development, and I had a very unlikely teacher who showed me a perspective of my students that would forever change the way I saw children.

Being twenty-four years old and forty-three kilometers from Tokyo was a perfect combination for excitement and new experiences. No rite of passage that significant would be complete without a road dog, a partner in crime, and a sister-friend. Mine was Sharita.

My third day in Japan, I received an email stating that there were several FAMU-ans in the Tokyo area. Like any true Rattler would do, I immediately reached out to one of them and planned a meeting in Yokohama. When I arrived, the young lady I met with told me that another FAMU-an would be joining us. Lo and behold, it was Sharita, a classmate of mine from college. I remembered her from when she visited my roommate in our dorm room freshman year. Sharita and I became fast friends.

Being a teacher for the Department of Defense was truly the best of both worlds. I had a beautiful beach house in Hayama, but I still enjoyed the comforts of home that the naval base provided. Sharita, on the other hand, was interning for a Fortune 500 company in Tokyo but couldn't get a box of Fruit Loops or her hair done in her neck of the woods. Needless to say, she would visit me quite often.

On one day in particular, she decided to volunteer in my class. I went about my daily routine of instructing students, reviewing classwork, and correcting behaviors. Sharita, being the funny lady she is, narrated my students' behaviors and conversations, giving each one a personality and a voice as if they were our age, with opinions and thoughts about everything around them:

> "He just asked me how to spell nocturnal. Girl, he is using nocturnal in his paragraph at seven years old. Kevin is going to be running a Fortune 500 in about thirty years. That's alright!"

> "Aww, Miss Hadley. Abigail loves you. She watches your every move just smiling. Girl, you are in here touching lives."

In that moment, I stepped outside of my routine as a classroom teacher and began to look at my students as individuals—funny, charming, witty, opinionated, and sometimes sarcastic individuals. I learned that although my students may not be able to articulate everything on their little minds as adults do, they had opinions and a right to be heard. From that day forward, I stopped teaching students and started nurturing and encouraging young people. That year, I first learned lessons that later empowered me to become my son's fiercest advocate.

ADVOCACY IN ACTION

MY SECOND YEAR teaching in Japan, I befriended a family—Miss Raejeana and her son, Shannon. Shannon was a middle-schooler, full of energy and life. Miss Raejeana was a single mother teaching early childhood education at the elementary schools on the naval base. At the time, she was in her late fifties. I was twenty-five, and Shannon was about twelve, so we were a bit of a motley crew, but they became my family that year. Every day after school I would go to Miss Raejeana's house and eat dinner with her family. She was a mother in the truest sense of the word. She cared for her son spiritually, physically, and mentally. She LOVED that child.

Shannon was my first intimate relationship with a child who had additional needs as well as my first introduction to an older child on an Individualized Education Program (IEP). Miss Raejeana was Shannon's advocate. I watched her work with him. I watched her work with the school system. And I watched her create every possible opportunity for Shannon to be successful. I didn't know it at the time, but God had positioned me in their home and in their family to prepare me to be a mother to my future son. I was able to see firsthand a mother's love and advocacy at work through Shannon and Miss Raejeana's relationship. I would sit at their dinner table and hear Miss Raejeana ask Shannon questions about his day. I would listen to her invoke higher-order thinking and prepare him for social and academic situations that many parents and children may take for granted. I watched Shannon struggle with fitting in at school. And I watched Miss Raejeana explain to him that he was perfectly formed.

I was able to sit in on that family and gather tools that I would later use in my own household with my own son. Shannon and Miss Raejeana taught me a lesson that year: that parents—not circumstances, not teachers, not communities, but parents—are the greatest influence on whether a child achieves success or falls between the cracks.

At the time, I was very young, not yet a mother, and had never had parents who were advocates for my well-being, so I didn't fully understand all of Miss Raejeana's behaviors. Sometimes I thought Miss Raejeana's actions for her son were a bit extreme. I would watch her go to the school and fuss and carry on because she felt as though Shannon had not been given a fair shake. I would think, *She's making a pretty big deal over something so small.* I couldn't possibly understand that Miss Raejeana, in that moment, for her twelve-year-old who was on the spectrum, was paving the ground for him to attend college, paving the ground for him to feel good about himself, paving the ground for him to know that he could come to her for any and everything, paving the ground for him to understand... *I got you, and I'm on your team.* She was his number one advocate and his greatest cheerleader.

I remember one day I came to Miss Raejeana's house after

school and found her fighting mad. She couldn't have been any more than one hundred pounds, but she was a pistol, especially when it came to her son. A teacher had given Shannon a grade that Miss Raejeana felt he didn't deserve because the teacher had not communicated to her that there had been a problem. She fully understood that some things presented a challenge to Shannon, and she was willing to do whatever work it took to make sure Shannon was successful. She felt cheated that this teacher had not given her the chance to create a successful opportunity for her son.

She went to that school and let them have it:

"I am the team captain when it comes to my child. Whatever is going on here, I need to know about. When I call and ask you how is he doing, give me a true and accurate answer. If he is struggling, let me know. If he needs to pay closer attention in class, let me know. If I don't know, I can't help. Please don't tell me my child is doing okay when he isn't. Sparing my feelings does not help my baby."

From that moment forward, those teachers knew she meant business when it came to her son.

Tick Tock Goes the Clock

AT TWENTY-FIVE YEARS old, living in Japan, footloose and fancy-free, I didn't think I had a care in the world. Finally, finally, finally I reached a point in my life where I had money in my pocket. I had a job that I enjoyed. I had a social life that was booming. Things couldn't get any more perfect in my world.

I was partying and having a good time, really not thinking about the future or about having a family. I spent a lot of time with a girlfriend, Denise, and despite her being six years older than me, I thought our feelings about the future were the same. One day when we were out, she suddenly broke down into tears. I'd never seen Denise cry, let alone sob. She was so fun-loving, full of energy. She lived in the moment. She was what I wanted to be, so needless to say, I was taken aback.

"What's going on?" I asked her.

She said, "I'm turning thirty-one tomorrow."

"I know," I said. "We're going to go to Tokyo, and we're going to celebrate your birthday and have an epic time." I went on and on about what a great time her thirty-first birthday was going to be. But her tears wouldn't stop.

Denise was active duty, unmarried, and a nurse. Her job was to deliver healthy babies every day, to put babies in the arms of their mothers and watch as they gave their new child warm, loving kisses. Despite the beauty in her job, Denise knew some things that weren't as warm and fuzzy.

"I'm telling you," she said. "You just don't understand. After thirty-one, I only have a couple more years to have a child before I become a high-risk pregnancy. So many women go about their lives and have fun and get an education and X, Y, and Z, but they forget that if you want to have a baby, it's something you need to plan for. If you want to be a mother, it doesn't just happen. It gets increasingly more difficult after a certain age."

This was the first time I was hearing about a biological clock. In the world I came from, babies *did* just kind of happen. You went about your business, and if you weren't careful, a baby would show up. I'd never had a friend who was at the stage of planning to be married or planning to have babies, or one who even wanted to have babies yet. That day, Denise made an impact on me. When I returned home, I decided, "I am twenty-five and need to change now. I am going to enjoy my life, but in thirty-six months, I'm going to be married."

I absolutely loved living in Japan. In addition to loving the country itself and the beauty and activities that were available to me right outside my door, I really loved the location of my home. I lived in a beautiful beach house in Hayama. Looking at Mount Fuji and the sunset every day made coming home probably one of the most peaceful experiences I've ever experienced to date.

When I found this perfect beach house on this perfect beach with this perfect view of Mount Fuji and this perfect position to receive the orange and red sunset every day, it was during the summer. I discovered that living here in the winter months was a different story. I felt as though I was living in a tinfoil house. The wind from the ocean would blow into my home, and it felt like I was standing outside. It became so cold that I stopped taking nightly showers and started taking my showers in the morning—nightly showers meant that I would be unable to get my feet to warm back up. The house had no central heating, just two little units on the walls, one for the first floor and one for the second, and they didn't do a good job of heating up the house. Needless to say, this Florida girl, after a second winter in Japan, just couldn't take it anymore.

There were some houses that were closer to the school where I taught that were a little more modern, *and* they had the amenities that would allow me to be warm in the winter. However, Japan has rules where you must pay the first and last month's rent, plus a gratuity to the land owner in order to move into a new unit. It would have cost me about $7,000 just to move five miles up the street. That wasn't going to happen. The military housing wasn't an option for me either because I didn't have any children or dependents. It was cheaper for me to put in a transfer to another country, so that's what I did.

The Department of Defense has a transfer program for its teachers. Every year, teachers get an opportunity to move from country to country, from school to school, to different class-rooms, different job opportunities based on need. When teachers move, resign, or retire, other teachers in other countries get an opportunity to fill those positions. When I put in my transfer request, I thought of South Korea. I had some friends who lived there. The country had everything I needed—great shopping, great food, public transportation, and most importantly, heated floors! When I finally received my transfer assignment, talk about excitement! Not only was I going to South Korea, I was going to Seoul.

I Want a Family

HOW WOULD I describe Seoul? Think about the liveliest college campus you could ever visit—fraternities, sororities, parties, dances, barbecues, fish fries. Now multiply that by one hundred. That was Seoul, South Korea. Seoul was an unaccompanied tour for the military personnel. An unaccompanied tour lasted about a year, with most of the service members coming without their families. There were married people, single people—most living alone. So community was a large part of Seoul. We got together quite often.

It was very easy to get caught up in the life of Seoul because there was something going on every weekend. I went to clubs on Friday nights, sorority meetings or activities on Saturday mornings and parties on Saturday nights, and church on Sunday mornings. I would have a fish fry after church or some get-together. Then during the weeks, I would have a date at this restaurant, a date at that restaurant, attend a cookout at a friend's house. In between all of the fun, I taught school and worked as an English Language Consultant.

Before I knew it, nearly six months had passed. In that time, I hadn't once thought about my conversation and experience with Denise a year prior. Then one day in January, I decided to go to the hair salon. I generally went to the hair salon on Wednesdays at 3:00 p.m., right after school. During this time, the salon was generally very quiet. But because I was on winter break, I decided to go in on a weekend at 10:00 in the morning.

The hair salon looked very different this day, full of mothers and their daughters having mommy-and-daughter time and getting ready for their weekend. I remember looking around that salon and watching these mothers and children interact with each other. I realized, in all my partying, in all my good time, I had lost sight of something that was very important to me. I had decided the year before that if I turned twenty-nine and wasn't married and didn't have a child, I would have a child on my own. I don't think I ever really thought about whether or not I *really* wanted to be a wife, but I knew I wanted to be a mother. However, as I watched the dads drop off their daughters and wives and give them kisses before leaving, I felt as though my child deserved to have two parents. I sat in my chair in the middle of the salon and began to cry.

A lady who was sitting nearby looked at me and said, "You have a light. Why are you sad?"

"I'm sad because I'm seeing all these moms with their daughters and all these dads dropping off their children and their wives, and I'm realizing I want that. I really, really want that, and I haven't done anything to work toward it."

She told me she believed I was going to have everything I wanted in life because I was able to say, "That's what I want." She continued, "So many people aren't able to say aloud, 'I want to be married, and I want to have a child.' That takes courage." She believed because I was able to say what I wanted at such a young age, it was going to happen for me and she poured into my spirit by telling me so. Through my tears, I smiled.

Once the seed of my desire had been officially planted, I saw the world around me differently. I saw dating differently. Although I had some bad habits in dating, sometimes choosing the wrong guys, other times staying in relationships longer than I should, I still had the seed—my desire to be a mother and wife—and I held it close.

One day when I came home from work, I followed my usual routine. I unlocked the door, went into my room, and pressed the button on my answering machine as I took off my shoes and unwound from the day.

"Hey, are we going to get together this weekend?"

"Hey, lady. Just checking in to see how you were doing."

"El'Tanya Patrice, this is your MeMe. Call home when you get a chance."

"Patrice, this is your Aunt Cassie. Give me a call as soon as you get home. I'm here with Mom."

I had been living overseas for about three years, and I'd never felt far away from my family until that moment—I immediately knew something was wrong. Why was everyone at my grandmother's house? My aunt lived in Tennessee. Why was she in Florida? This was in a time before international calls were simple, so in order to call back to the United States, I had to press several buttons: my calling card number, the number that I was calling, *press one for this, press two for that*. My brain could not think. It took me over ten minutes to call home.

When I finally got through, my grandmother answered the phone.

"Hey. What's wrong? What's going on?" I asked.

She said, "Baby, Ralph Daniels has been killed."

My mind wasn't working well at this point. I was flustered. My grandfather's name was Ralph Daniels, Sr. My uncle's name was Ralph Daniels, Jr. My cousin's name was Ralph Daniels III. I did not know who she was referring to. I said, "MeMe. Who – who – who has been killed?"

"Your Uncle Ralph," she answered.

I felt my breath leave my body. Uncle Ralph had been my surrogate father. My biological father had been a very inconsistent presence in my life. I hadn't even met him until I was about six years old. He wasn't really, in my opinion, father material. He didn't work consistently. He didn't keep his word. He was not what I would want for my child as a father. But I was fortunate enough to have my Uncle Ralph. In many of those instances where a father should have been there, my Uncle Ralph was there instead. At my high school graduation, he was there. On my prom night, he was there. For my college graduation, he was there. And he was there when I brought home my first serious guy.

Now, to hear on a phone call, seven thousand miles away, that my Uncle Ralph was no longer with us was more than I could take. My family wanted to have a quick funeral, and because I was so far away, they felt it was best I stayed in Korea and worked. By the time I found a flight out from Korea to Florida, got there for the funeral and came back, they felt it might be a little more on me than I should have to handle as a single woman. So I didn't attend the funeral.

During that time, I finally realized I was alone in a foreign country. My mind began to play games with me at night. What if I died on a Friday after school? If someone didn't hear from me Friday night, they would think I had chosen to stay in. If someone didn't hear from me on Saturday morning, they would think I had chosen to have some time in solitude, which I often did. If they didn't see me at church or hear from me on Sunday, maybe they'd think I had met someone. Monday morning, if I didn't show in to work, the first thought wouldn't be "Is she okay?" but probably "She's being irresponsible." They'd get a substitute in my room and try to call me. But it wouldn't be until Tuesday that someone might say, "Hey, we need to go to her house and see if she is okay." That would be concern coming from my job—not family, not friends, but my job. I had managed to move halfway around the world, socialize with people, have fun, but I had built walls around myself because I enjoyed my privacy. With the passing of my uncle Ralph, I realized in setting these boundaries and enjoying this privacy, I had not established a family.

I don't remember being functional at work that week, but I do remember one of my students looking at me with concern in his eyes.

"Richard, I'm okay. Get back to work."

"Miss Hadley, you don't look okay."

Soon I had an influx of parents sending food and flowers and well-wishes. They had all heard of my uncle's passing. Then one day I was in my classroom, standing and looking at my students, all of a sudden unable to breathe. I went into the classroom of the teacher next to me. She was in a private room because she worked with small groups of students, and there were no students with her then.

I said, "I think I need to call 911. I feel like I'm losing my mind."

I was taken to the emergency room. After the doctor checked my vitals, he asked me, "When is the last time you slept?"

I realized I had not slept a full night in over a week because I had been so worried about mortality.

He told me, "Miss Hadley, I need you to go home. Take these sleeping pills and just rest. You've had a panic attack. It's pretty common, and you've gone through a traumatic life experience. You need to rest."

A friend took me home, and another friend came by to watch over me as I took the pills. For the first time since my uncle's passing, I had a full night's sleep.

In a military hospital, when you have something like a panic attack, they suggest you make an appointment with a psychiatrist. On May 25, I got up for my appointment and went to meet with the military psychiatrist. I sat in his office as he asked me a series of questions. I listened to him and began thinking, *Wow. He has absolutely no bedside manner. I am so uncomfortable right now. He's asking me extremely personal questions but not seeking to establish a rapport at all.* Needless to say, I couldn't get out of his office fast enough. I walked downstairs and hailed a cab in the pouring rain. Many people walk in Seoul, so on rainy days the cabs are in full swing, and traffic is a nightmare. We sat at the light. One minute. Two minutes. Three minutes. Four minutes. Five minutes passed by, and I began to feel like I was trapped in the back of the cab. I decided to pay my cab fare, get out, and walk home in the rain.

The rain pouring down on my head seemed to mask my tears as I walked home. My head was spinning. Where had I gotten in life that I was in a psychiatrist's office looking for answers as opposed to getting on my knees and praying? I'd been through a lot in my twenty-seven years of life. Ups, downs, in betweens. Experienced things I wouldn't wish on my worst enemy. But I was always able to come out on the other end because of my relationship with God. Now I had a little money and a comfortable life, and He had answered all of my prayers, but I had forgotten that He was my confidante and could help me find my way.

When I got home, I opened the door, and in my wet clothes, dripping from the rain, I fell to my knees and prayed.

"Lord, I want a family more than anything in this world. I want someone to call my own. I want someone who is there for me. I want a child to love, to protect, to care for. I am so thankful for all You have given me. You have given me more than I ever thought I would have. If a family and a child is not what You want me to have, Lord, I pray for You to take that desire from my heart and allow me to be content with the blessings You have given me. I can't do this on my own. I've tried and failed. I give it all to You."

After I got up from my knees that day in May, I felt as though a weight had been lifted. I put all my problems on the altar, so all I had to do was let my light shine and live my life. I had a great career, a great home, a great social life, so what did I do next? Grad school. I had no desire to be a principal or an administrator. However, teachers don't get merit-based pay. We move across the pay scale as we increase in academic achievement, and we move down the pay scale by years in education in the classroom. The only way for me to get a raise in teaching, a significant raise, was to either teach more years or get more education.

I applied and was accepted to the University of Southern Mississippi. That summer I was going to spend some time in Hattiesburg, Mississippi. I left immediately following the end of the school year. I had a wonderful time in Hattiesburg and thoroughly enjoyed the university. I came out that summer with a 4.0 GPA, ready to start my fall classes and my summer in my international cohorts program. I felt completely motivated, rejuvenated, and optimistic about life.

When classes were over, I was supposed to stay for a couple more days in Hattiesburg to see a friend of mine graduate. But as a grown woman accustomed to having her own space, the dorm room was really taking a toll on me. I decided to bump up my flight to the very next day and head back to Korea. I had a very uneventful plane trip from Biloxi to Atlanta, Atlanta to Seoul. After landing in Seoul and going to the baggage claim, I discovered my luggage was stuck in Atlanta. Luckily, I had my party clothes and other essentials in my carry-on bag.

My friend, Duane, picked me up from the airport, took me home, and my girlfriends met me there. I dyed my hair and got prettied up, and we headed off to enjoy a night on the town. While out, one of my sorority sisters, Caryn, met a guy and took a fancy to him. He would never have been the guy I would have chosen for her, but she was getting over a break-up, and he seemed to be quite interested in her.

That night, my first night back in Korea, we partied until 1:00 in the morning. When we returned to my house, we crashed. The next morning we decided to head out into the city. After a fun day of shopping, we went back to my house to relax. We talked and laughed until we eventually fell asleep, exhausted from our adventures.

The doorbell woke us up from our naps at 10:30 at night. Thankfully, someone from Korean Air was at the door, bringing my luggage. I thanked him, tipped him, and brought my things inside. Now Caryn and I were wide awake. Because she was getting over a break-up, I was worried the topic of her ex-boyfriend would come up. I was not prepared to have that conversation again, so I quickly said, "Hey, why don't we get dressed and go out dancing or to a club on post?"

We decided to go to a club called The Underground, on the US Army installation. Caryn was hesitant about this club at first because The Underground was a club for enlisted service members only. As a young military officer, she was worried of getting in trouble for going, but I convinced her: "Let's just go, and we can sit on the wall and not really talk to anybody. We'll just listen to the music and enjoy the night."

We arrived and did as I suggested. My spirits were up. I saw friends I hadn't seen all summer. Caryn and I happened to look up at the same time and see the guy she had taken a liking to the night before. As the dutiful "wingman" I was, I called the guy and his friend over.

It was my job as wingman to distract the guy's friend so Caryn could have some privacy with the object of her affection. So I took the friend out on the dance floor. I had no interest in this guy, but as we were dancing, he looked down at me and said, "Maybe I should come to Seoul more often."

Did he really just use that line on me?

We ended our time on the dance floor, but he continued to hang around. I ended up talking to him more that night and giving him my number, but when it was time to go, we said our good-byes, and I really didn't give him much thought after that. The next day, I got a phone call from him, and things just kind of took off from there. Because Korean Air forgot my bags, I met a guy with a super corny line who eventually stole my heart.

The young officer and I began the most wonderful courtship. One of the reasons our courtship was so special was because it took place in Korea. As I explained earlier, Seoul was an unaccompanied, one-year tour, and most of the military personnel took it without dependents. Therefore, Seoul was definitely a party environment. So, meeting a young man who was serious about dating was a bit of an anomaly. Everything was right about him, but something held me back. Did I deserve someone this nice? Could he be genuine? He must have some skeletons hidden in his closet somewhere, because stuff like this didn't happen to girls like me.

Then one night he told me he loved me. I thought about it for a moment. He was so kind and so good to me. I said, "I love you too." And I meant it—I meant that he was a great guy. He treated me well, and for that I loved him. But he was in love, and I was not. I didn't know how to be in love. I'd never had a good model for true love, but I loved him in a general sort of way, as best I could. Our relationship grew, and he continued to shower me with an affection and regard I had never known before.

One day I was on my way to school. I always parked across the street from the school and crossed at the crosswalk. But this day was different. There was a little girl in front of me with her dad, dressed in his uniform. I watched them as they walked across the street. The little girl turned and looked at her dad with the most sincere look of adoration I had ever seen in my life. Her eyes and her face communicated that she felt as though this man was the greatest man in the world. I'd never experienced that feeling as a child. In that moment, I knew with 100 percent certainty that the young officer I was dating would be the man who would ensure that my children would experience what that little girl felt. It was then that I fell in love. I still felt I didn't deserve him, but I knew by choosing him I would give my future children the greatest gift a mother could ever give—a wonderful father.

WITH CHILD

A COUPLE YEARS into our marriage, we relocated to Lawton, Oklahoma for eight months so my husband could attend an Officer Career Course. Lawton was a small city with only two major streets, but each street was lined with several restaurants. In truth, the only things to do in Lawton were go to work and eat. We had a small one-bedroom apartment, and we made the most of it. It was a huge contrast from where I'd been just a year ago, but we were together after a year-long deployment, and that's all that mattered.

Every Sunday morning, we got dressed and went to church. All the families were well-dressed. I had a weakness in particular for the little girls with ribbons in their hair. There was something about a little girl with ribbons in her hair that said, "I am well cared for." I longed to care for a child.

One Sunday, my husband and I were sitting in the pew, listening to the children's choir, and as I watched the children, something so powerful moved within me. It was that seed again, that strong desire that said, *I want a baby.*

I had actually started birth control some months earlier because, after being separated from my husband for a year due to a deployment to Iraq, I wanted to enjoy our time together.

I said we could focus on a baby later. And now, I really didn't think it was fair to say I had suddenly changed my mind. So I prayed about it. I didn't want to bring it up to him, because I knew he wanted to focus on his career for a few years, and I didn't think now was the ideal time for a baby. But though I kept my words to myself, I wasn't good at hiding my feelings. I cried on the altar every Sunday. Eventually my husband got the hint.

One day after church, he got on one knee yet again and asked me to have his baby. Being the Type-A personality that I am, I decided if we were going to try, we were going to do it right. "Okay," I said. "Let's go to the store now. Let's get an ovulation kit. Let's buy books and do research. I have to prepare my body to conceive."

But all it took was me, my husband, and some slow jams. The next month, my cycle didn't come. Five o'clock one morning, I woke up because I was a day late. After my husband left for work, I got in the car and went to a twenty-four hour store and bought a pregnancy test. I went home and took the test— it was positive. I decided to surprise my husband with the news, so I got dressed, grabbed his lunch, and bought a baby rattle to put inside his lunchbox. I went to the military installation to meet him for lunch, and when he opened his lunchbox, he saw the baby rattle.

"We're having a baby!" I said.

We were ecstatic, but I realized I needed to make a doctor's appointment. I left lunch and went directly to the hospital to show someone my positive pregnancy test. Amused, the nurse looked at me and essentially said, "Hey, Lady. I know you're excited but I can't read this. This is a store-bought pregnancy test. We have to do our own." So I took one of their pregnancy tests and was told I would be called with the results.

I got the call, which pretty much said that the tests were inconclusive, and I needed to wait a little while longer, maybe three, four days and come back again, because either it was too early to tell or I was pregnant.

Those were the longest four days of my life. Finally, I went back to the hospital, full of hope, and took another pregnancy test. We were out looking for a house for our new baby when we got the call. The results were positive. I don't think it was possible to be more excited than we were in that moment. I did a happy dance right there in the realtor's office, and we called and shared the news with everyone under the sun. We were going to have a baby!

At six weeks, something didn't feel right. I went to the bathroom to check myself and found thick blood, and a lot of it. A sense of dread filled me as we got in the car and drove to the emergency room. We waited for what felt like an eternity. I didn't understand why I was not a priority to the doctors. This was my baby, my world. But to the world, I was just an early-term pregnancy.

Three or more hours passed before I was finally taken into a room. While the doctor looked for a heartbeat, I prepared myself for the worst. He asked my husband, "What do you see?"

My husband said, "I see a heartbeat."

"Look again. What else do you see?"

My husband said, "Two heartbeats!" with a laugh of relief.

I had gone from being pregnant to thinking I was having a

miscarriage to being pregnant with twins. I was over the moon. My shouts of praise could be heard throughout the ER.

However, during our next doctor's visit, we were told I had several clots that were co-existing with our babies. Because of that, they wanted to give me progesterone and put me on modified bedrest to ensure that the clots didn't take over my pregnancy.

When we went in for yet another checkup a few weeks later, something was wrong. My husband stood beside the table and held my hand as we waited for the doctor. Finally she came in, and after a little small talk, she began her checkup. She looked at the monitor and then smiled at me. I smiled back and watched her turn her face back to the monitor. This time she looked concerned. When she asked to be excused, I began to panic. I squeezed my husband's hand and said a prayer. When the doctor reentered, she was accompanied by another, older doctor. They both checked me and then examined the monitor together. The woman doctor pointed to a hollow black spot on the monitor, and he gave her a solemn nod.

"Twin B has a strong heartbeat, but Twin A has not grown since your last visit."

My breath left my body.

I was devastated. I'd planned a life for my babies. Now one of them was gone. It had to be a mistake. I made them check again and said a prayer. God had to answer prayers. But it was no mistake. I lay still as tears rolled down my face. My heart was broken.

We left the hospital in silence. I settled in at home and prepared for full bedrest. The arrogance of youth, of having twins our first time trying, was gone. I spent the next five months bargaining with God.

"Father, if You see fit to deliver this child safely to my arms, I promise on everything in me that I will protect and nurture his soul. I know he is Yours, but if you just let me borrow him on earth, I promise I will protect and love him with everything in me. I will be the best mother ever. Grant me Your mercy."

About five months into the pregnancy and after several doctor's appointments, we went back in for yet another checkup on Twin B, but something in the test wasn't reading well.

The doctor told me, "Your baby may have Down's syndrome. You can have an amniocentesis or a Level 3 ultrasound."

She explained the risks involved. We decided to go with the Level 3 ultrasound because the rate of miscarriage with an amniocentesis was greater than the chances of having a child with Down's syndrome. Down's syndrome was the least of my concerns at that point because we just wanted our baby safe and here with us. We went for the ultrasound a few weeks later and saw a perfectly formed baby boy. He was even giving me a little thumb's up, as if to say, "Hey, mom. It's all good."

Once we got home and I was settled in my recliner, my husband prepared to go back to work. As he headed for the door, I called out to him. "Hey, you forgot to take the sonogram picture." I was sure he would want to show the picture of his son to the other soldiers in his unit.

He responded, "No, I'll leave it here. I'll just keep some things to myself."

I heard his words… but I read his eyes. He was tired. This had been a long and emotional pregnancy. Not what either of us had envisioned. His pregnant wife didn't show up at his job with lunch. We didn't get to go to church each Sunday and have the members says, "Oh, that's going to be a boy because she's carrying low" or "Oh, how beautiful! Your wife is just glowing." Our pregnancy was filled with tears, fears, scary doctor visits, bedrest, and medication. And because I had gotten pregnant and placed on bedrest so soon after arriving in Oklahoma, we had not had the opportunity to make many friends. So we were pretty isolated in our one-bedroom apartment. I could see in his eyes that the innocence of hope was gone. My heart sank, but I knew I had enough hope for the both of us.

I gave him a faint smile, the best I could manage, and said, "Okay, I understand. I'll see you when you get home."

My Heart Outside of My Body

MY HUSBAND GRADUATED, and at seven months pregnant I was cleared for travel. We had orders to Monterey, California, for eighteen months of graduate school. I was excited. I'd been given a clean bill of health. My pregnancy was going well. My husband was about to go to graduate school, and we were going to be able to spend some time together for the next eighteen months.

When we arrived in Monterey, we immediately found a doctor. This doctor was different from the military doctors I had grown accustomed to. He had a bedside manner that made me feel comfortable, and he even made jokes during my visits to help lighten the mood. One time he said my baby was perfectly formed but that we just needed to leave him in there a little longer so he could fully "bake in mom's oven."

I was beginning to feel like a regular pregnant woman. I went about my daily life—finding a home, making a home, helping my husband prepare for school, cooking dinner, doing laundry, everything. And I was truly happy.

About four days before my due date, we had a doctor's appointment. We found out my baby boy was breached, bottom down with his arms and legs at the top of my belly. The doctor gave us a few options. We could have the baby turned, but it would be a very painful procedure with a fifty percent chance the baby would turn back to his current position. We could wait and go into labor, but we would have to call the ambulance, and I would have to ride to the hospital on all fours because anything else could compress the umbilical cord and cut off air to my baby. Or, I could have a caesarian.

I didn't like any of those options. None of them fit with what I had planned. My husband and I were currently taking Lamaze classes. I had my birthing ball, candles, everything a pregnant woman needed. I had the music we were going to play as my husband held my hand and coached me through our practiced breathing and methods. We had done all the right things. We thought we were ready. But nothing was going as planned.

After that appointment, I drove my husband back to school. I held a brave face, but I was completely devastated and afraid, for me and my baby. Everything seemed to be pointing to a C-section. But I had never had a surgery. What if I didn't make it? Who was going to be a mother to my son? I felt completely lost. I couldn't go home. I couldn't be alone.

I had a friend, a classmate from college, whose mother happened to be in town. I decided to drive to his house to see her. She greeted me warmly at the door, and I went to their dining room table and cried. She made me a sandwich, sat next to me, and listened as I explained the doctor's visit and my options.

"What do I do?" I asked her. "I'm so afraid." She asked me what I wanted to do. I said, "I just want to get him here safely."

She replied, "Then that's what you do."

She was so comforting. She gave me a hug and rubbed my back. We talked about life and babies and motherhood. When I left, I felt at ease. I felt warm. I felt safe. And I remember thinking, *Is that what it feels like to have a mother? I can't wait to be a mom.*

I told my husband I was okay with the caesarian. It might not have been the plan, but it was the quickest way to get our baby safely to our arms.

Our baby was due on September 22, my birthday. We scheduled the caesarian for September 20. Like any doctor visit, we went in. We knew the procedure, but this doctor's visit was going to be a little different—we were going to come out with a baby! I got dressed in my hospital gear and was given all the medicine I needed for comfort. I had to wait a little while longer because they had an emergency caesarian on our floor. At four in the afternoon, they rolled me into the operating room. My husband came in, and the process of bringing our baby into this world began. I was so anxious. When they finally pulled him out, I didn't hear anything, and for a moment I was afraid. Then all of a sudden I heard the most beautiful sound I'd ever heard. My baby's cry!

On that table, belly wide open, I started giving praises to my God at the top of my lungs. "Thank you, Father God. Thank you. You are so wonderful. I appreciate all that you've done for me, Father God. Oh, Father God, thank you."

I think I scared the anesthesiologist. I heard her say, "What's wrong with her?"

My doctor said, "She's just giving praises to God. She's happy. Her son is here."

I didn't get to see my son right way, since I was lying flat on my back on the table. My husband put our baby in my face, but I didn't have my glasses on, so I only remember seeing lots of black hair and a gray blur. Next thing I knew, they whisked our son away, and my husband followed. They rolled me to the recovery room, and as soon as my husband joined me, I began asking him a series of questions.

"What does he look like? Did you see his little toes? Does he have a lot of hair? Is he big? Is everything okay? My goodness, what is taking them so long?"

My husband answered in a calm, reassuring voice, "He's beautiful. He's perfect. And everything is okay."

Moments later, the nurse pushed in a bassinet full of perfection. As they put him in my arms, I cried tears of joy. He latched on to me, and in that moment I felt peace, joy, gratitude, and the most primal sense of the need to protect that I had ever felt in my life. My son, Ricky II, was born on Wednesday, September 20, 2006, and so was Mama Bear.

Because of my caesarian, we spent four days in the hospital. I had the nurses coming in to wait on me and to help us with our baby. I could call a nurse if anything concerned me, so I became pretty comfortable. But after day four, when it was time for me to be discharged, I got a little nervous. I thought, *Okay, so, they're actually going to let us just take this baby home with us?* Despite all our classes and preparation, I didn't know what to do, and neither did my husband. I was so glad my grandmother would be coming to visit.

Once we arrived home with our baby, my husband left to pick up my grandmother from the airport. After he left, I realized I hadn't changed diapers while our baby was in the hospital, and diaper changing was a little different with a real live baby than with the doll we had practiced on in class. Fortunately, one of my sorority sisters came to the house and taught me how to change the diaper on a moving baby and how to wrap the used diaper up neatly. And so began my time with my Super Duper Kid.

INTRO TO MAMAHOOD

THE FIRST MONTH with Ricky II was pretty typical. We were exhausted parents, up all night, learning to breastfeed, learning to take care of a little person, and trying to adjust to our new normal. Now our family consisted of Ricky II, my husband, myself, and the dog. Everything was going pretty well. I was finding my rhythm, a little tired but more excited than anything. We had a co-sleeper, a little bassinet that sat next to the bed, and we attached it to the bottom of the mattress so that he was right beside me.

When Ricky II was about four weeks old, I was still in recovery, but my body just wasn't feeling the way it normally felt. The caesarian had been my first surgery, and I was very aware the doctor had opened me up and taken a baby out of my body. Because of my pregnancy, I had gotten to the point where I didn't trust my body anymore. We no longer had a relationship. I felt as though my body had failed me on so many levels while I was carrying my son that I was afraid of what could happen to me on any given day. I had two major car accidents in my early twenties, and sciatic nerve pain throughout my pregnancy, so I wasn't very mobile after Ricky II was born. That had me feeling really down because I had previously been very active. When I was teaching school, I was very hands-on with the students. I spent a lot of time on the floor, rolling around with my kids. I could even remember rolling down hills in Japan on field trips.

Now I had this baby, and it hurt for me to get out of a chair. I had tinglings in my hand and wrist, and I didn't know why. I thought again of my uncle's passing and how I had been so concerned with mortality. I made an appointment with the doctor, a primary care physician through our insurance company. When I went to see him, I began telling him all the symptoms I was having and how I was feeling. How I wanted to feel like myself again, but I was at a really low point because I'd had a baby, and after a month, I still didn't feel as though I was operating at one hundred percent.

I was reaching out for something, and I don't know exactly what it was, but that doctor wasn't giving it to me. He listened to me talk, and then he looked at me and asked, "Have you always been chubby?"

I was completely taken aback. I thought, *Wow. Where do you go from there?*

I gathered up my baby, left the office, and got in my car. My husband was in school, so I couldn't reach him. My grandmother had already left town. I realized I was alone and started to cry.

Then I remembered when we were taking our maternity photos and when we were at Lamaze class, people had been speaking of an organization called Parents' Place that was in the Pacific Grove community. They said Parents' Place was a safe place for new parents to go that would teach me the things I needed to do with my little one.

I left the doctor's office and drove to Parents' Place with tears in my eyes. I got my baby out the car, went in, and said, "Hi. My name's El. This is my baby, Ricky II. I need help."

Parents' Place has a policy—where if you had a baby between zero and three months, they never turned you away. I enrolled and started classes. In our first class, the parents met, and we sang to our babies with the accompaniment of a local artist. I remember crying because I was now in a room with other mothers and their babies, no longer at home by myself.

Parents' Place had core classes. Our class met once a week. The mothers would sit around a circle with our little ones and sing and share stories. I was participating in a Mommy and Me program. This program built a community for me, and it built a community for my son. I had a support group. I had friends. I had family. I had other women who were going through the exact same things I was going through. We were able to talk to each other. Through this experience, I learned how to be a mommy.

I'm a huge, huge supporter of Mommy and Me and parent education because when someone puts a baby in your arms, no matter how much you want to do for that child, you don't know what you don't know. You have all these feelings going on inside of you, and you need an outlet to express those feelings. A happy mommy equals a happy baby. I thank God for the community that is offered in Mommy and Me classes.

By the time Ricky II was eleven months old, I had found my rhythm. I loved being his mama. Oh my goodness, we had full days every day. I had my Mommy and Me friends from Parents' Place. We would get together every single day and do something, whether it was a play date at someone's house, a walk in the park or on the trails, Stroller Strides, a Mommy and Me music class, a trip to the aquarium. You name it, we did it. We woke up every morning, and by 9:00 am, we were out having a grand old time. I absolutely loved being a mom, and I loved being a stay-at-home mom. But more than anything, I loved my son.

Mama Bear's First Growl

WHEN MY HUSBAND and I were dating, we had talked about what our family would look like. We had always said we would stair-step our children. I wanted three children. He wanted an even number of children because he didn't want anyone to feel on the outside at any given time, so we agreed on four kids. Now, at this point, I was thirty-one years old, so I figured we needed to get back into action. When Ricky II was eleven months old, we weren't really trying, but we weren't stopping it. Right before his first birthday, I found out I was pregnant. Our babies would be twenty-two months apart, and in about nine months, Ricky II was going to have a playmate in the house. I don't think I could have been any more excited.

I made an appointment with the OB-GYN after my doctor confirmed my pregnancy. We decided to take some precautions because I'd had a miscarriage with Twin A. I had started spotting, so I took it easy and abruptly stopped breastfeeding based on my doctor's suggestion. My pregnancy seemed to be going fine, but by week eleven, I wasn't feeling pregnant anymore. We went to the doctor, and he confirmed our baby hadn't grown since the last visit. There was no heartbeat.

I hadn't seen this coming. Although I had lost a child

during my pregnancy with Ricky II, I was told it was vanishing twin syndrome—it happens. But this time, there had been only one baby inside of me, and now that baby was gone. I didn't know what to do. Just like that, it was over.

Around Thanksgiving time, I was home recovering from a D&C (dilation and curettage) procedure, unable to see the things in front of me that I should be thankful for. To make matters worse, my husband told me that immediately after his graduation the next month, he would be leaving for Kansas to train for two months. After that, he would be off to Iraq for another year-long deployment.

While trying to process this information, I didn't know if I was coming or going. Just two weeks before I had been the happiest woman in the world. I had a perfect baby, another one on the way, and a husband. Now I'd had two miscarriages, and my husband was going to be deployed, and I was going to be faced with raising my son by myself for a year. I broke. Depression overcame me and I sat in our living room with the lights out and didn't leave the house for a full month.

My husband became concerned. We knew we had two months before he would actually have to go to Iraq, but in the interim, he had to go to Kansas for training. He decided he needed to take his family with him so we would not be alone during that time.

We packed up our bags, and in late December, we moved to Junction City, Kansas, Fort Riley. It was cold there. In addition to being cold, it was a very small city with little to do. I started to worry about what I was going to do with Ricky II. He was used to an active life. Despite my concerns, I was starting to feel a little better. I was with my family, and now that we were in a new environment, I didn't have any questions about my pregnancy. In Monterey, I had shared the news of our second pregnancy. I realized I had stayed in our house for a month because I hadn't wanted to answer questions about my pregnancy when I no longer had one. Now I was able to walk out of my house because no one in our new town knew that I had been pregnant and was no longer pregnant. That was something I didn't have to face. Junction City, Kansas, gave me a new lease on life.

Our family ventured out every weekend to do little things. Now that I watch videos of Ricky II and us then, I see that we filled in a lot of his blanks.

"Oh, look at Ricky II."

"There's Ricky II."

"Oh my gracious, Ricky II is awesome."

"Ricky II really likes this toy."

Ricky II just kind of hung out with us rather than interact with us. By this time, he was about sixteen months and wasn't walking yet, so I was carrying him. I knew this was something I should be concerned about, but he was such a delightful child that I felt he'd come around given time.

I wanted to make sure Ricky II stayed current on his doctor visits and that someone was keeping track of him, so I decided I would take him to a doctor on the base. Now this doctor, who had never seen my child before—he didn't know my child, didn't know me, didn't know our medical history— asked, "Is he talking?"

I said, "No."

"Is he walking?"

"No."

"And how old is he?"

"He's sixteen months."

"If you put him down on the floor, will he walk?"

"Nope."

"If you ask him to give you the red cup, can he give you the red cup?"

I said, "I've never asked him to give me a red cup."

"If he wants something to drink, can he say, 'Give me some water'?"

"No. He's never had to ask me to give him water. I'm there to take care of all his needs."

My son was sitting in my lap. The doctor instructed me, "Put him on the floor."

My baby didn't have on socks or shoes, and he was just in a diaper, but I did as instructed.

In this moment, almost eight years later, I regret that visit in ways I could never possibly put into words in a book. But I complied that day and put my baby on the floor.

The doctor clapped his hands together and said, "Come here, walk."

My baby just stood there holding my hand.

The doctor commanded again, "Walk. Walk."

I picked my child up and said, "He's not walking yet," and left.

When I got in my truck, I called my girlfriend and told her about the doctor's visit.

I said, "I feel like I failed him. I feel as though I did not protect him in that visit. The doctor's tone was too harsh. He was commanding my child to walk, and when Ricky II didn't do it, the doctor behaved as if Ricky was doing something wrong. I will never let that happen again. I will always protect my child." As Mama Bear, this was my first growl.

An upside of Junction City was that I had found a

wonderful Parents as Teachers playgroup, hosted by the city government. Twice a week I would take Ricky II to the play groups on the military installation and at the public library. We started to build a community and make friends. We were having a good time in Junction City. A month after moving there, Ricky II moved from an army crawl and cruising to walking. We were in a small studio apartment, so we took him for walks in the mall. He even learned to say the word "touch-down." Things were going well for us.

Something else happened in Junction City. Two months after we moved there, I found out I was pregnant again. Our family was about to be complete. We were going to have our next child and stop there. When my husband's training was over, we loaded in the truck and headed back to California. Ricky II was with me. My husband was with me. My dog was with me. Our baby was in my belly. Life was good!

After we arrived back in California, my husband spent one of his two days home before leaving for Iraq building a nice white picket fence around our beautiful home. While he was gone, I'd need a fence to keep Ricky II safely corralled in the yard while I had my arms full with our new bundle of joy. We drove my husband to the airport on the day he was set to leave, and I gave him a hug and a kiss and said good-bye for a year.

THE BIRTH OF AN ADVOCATE

LIFE MOVED PRETTY quickly after my husband left for Iraq. Ricky II was approaching eighteen months old, and he was as busy as ever. Now that he was walking—whoa, momma!—life had certainly changed. I was about eight weeks along, so I went to my first doctor's visits. This was the first doctor's appointment I'd had during a pregnancy without my husband. But my doctor took excellent care of me, and everything was just fine.

Life was good. I was taking care of Ricky II, and we'd reconnected with our friends. I'd told them I was pregnant and that things were going well for us—at least as well as they could with my husband thousands of miles away in Iraq.

I was back into my rhythm of being a mom and an expecting mom. One morning I was in serious multitask mode, getting ready for a doctor's appointment, feeding Ricky II breakfast, and packing up his things to take him to hourly care at the Child Development Center on base. While feeding Ricky II, I noticed he was looking at me, but there was something different in his eyes that day. It was like he was really seeing me for the first time. I stopped what I was doing, looked at him, and said, "You're so perfect. You are amazing, and I'm so happy to be your mommy. You are all I need in this world."

I had gone to the doctor two weeks earlier because I didn't feel pregnant, but I had a heartbeat, so everything seemed to be okay. My doctor had sat down with me and told me, "I know how much you want a child. We're going to do everything in our power to get your baby here and healthy, but remember, this is not on you. You can't will and hope a healthy baby here. It's God's will."

Now I was going for the visit that would bring me toward the close of my first trimester. I had a cake I had baked for my doctor in hand to thank him for his words of comfort during my last visit. I went into the examination room, got on the table, and found out that there wasn't a heartbeat. Our baby was gone.

Through my tears, I listened as my doctor said, "It is times like these that I have to draw closest to God. There are babies born every day to people who don't want to be parents, and when I sit next to someone who has prayed for a child and it doesn't happen, I just don't understand. But God's will is not for me to understand. I just pray that He gives me the words to comfort my patients." In that room, on that day, my doctor cried with me.

I was comforted by my doctor's words. I was not okay, but I was at peace.

This was my third miscarriage in two years. My husband had always been there to hold my hand. This one I was going to have to do alone. I cleaned myself off and got off the table. The nurse asked me if I wanted to call anyone since my husband was not there. I said, "No. I just have to go get my child."

I got in my car, drove to the CDC, and got my baby.

When we got home, I held him close to me. I was so grateful to be his mother.

Ricky II, and I were settling into our new routine. I was no longer pregnant, so it was just the two of us. Pregnancy was not something I could concern myself with for a while because my husband was gone and would be gone for quite some time, so I began to focus all of my attention on Ricky II. Now, granted, I had always focused a great deal of my attention on him, but I had a husband, and up until recently, it seemed like I always had a child on the way. I'd had so many things going on. But this time, I just wanted it to be me and Ricky II for a while.

We stopped participating in play dates for a while, so no additional language and conversation was around us. It was just the two of us. I began to notice something that I had not fully noticed before. If I wasn't talking, there was complete silence. There was absolutely no conversation in the house. None at all. I talked, and Ricky II listened, at least I thought he was listening, but he wasn't making any attempts to speak to me. I made an appointment with our doctor. When I took him in, I said, "My son's not speaking. He has a couple of words that he says, like 'hi,' 'bye,' 'touchdown,' but he's not making any attempts to communicate with me." At the doctor's recommendation, I quickly made an appointment with his pediatrician.

The doctor looked at him—he was healthy, fit as a fiddle—and said, "Children develop at different rates. Just keep doing what you're doing, mom—you're doing a great job— and watch him." Then he gave us a sticker.

That visit made me realize that, yes, I was a mom, but I'd also been a teacher. I'd worked with hundreds of students— evaluating them, assessing them, and referring them based on my observation to get the assistance that they needed. Now it was time for me to use my skill set for the benefit of the child that God had blessed me with. I realized in the past I had been intimidated in doctor's visits. Somehow I had convinced myself that someone else knew what was best for my child. I decided I would walk into his next doctor's visit armed with my objective observations and get to the root of what was going on with my child. After that visit, I stopped being just Ricky II's mom and started being his teacher because the onus was solely on me to build my case for my son's needs to be addressed and met.

When we got home, I started taking anecdotal notes. I wrote down everything. I researched what I could do to make a connection with my son. I knew that my son loved to learn; he just did it a little differently. He didn't necessarily pick up things contextually. I had to make a concerted effort in everything I did to make connections for my baby. I started talking constantly to him, pantomiming every word I said to ensure he would gather some meaning from all of the language I presented to him. I read countless articles on language development and making connections in young children.

I looked up kinesthetic activities because my son was constantly in motion. I found music that reinforced the language skills I was working to develop in him because he had a natural affinity to music. Ricky II loved to touch and feel everything around him, so I began to use colorful manipulatives made from household items to encourage him to explore as I taught and observed him. Once I conceptualized how my baby learned, I pulled all these elements together and developed a curriculum for him, which incorporated content-rich children's music and colorful and inviting manipulatives with movement-based learning activities.

We started with basic animals. If I were teaching him the word "lion," we would play with a fuzzy lion puppet, and I would roar and act like a lion on the floor. I would play Greg and Steve's Animal Action and we would dance around and pretend to be lions. I was on a mission to make as many connections as possible for my son. I was living the words that my assistant principal at Seoul American Elementary School told me after one of my teacher evaluations:

"Miss Hadley, you are a good teacher. I want you to be a great teacher. Good teachers can teach one hundred things one way. Great teachers can teach one thing one hundred ways so that every child has an opportunity to learn."

I didn't fully understand her words when she spoke them to me, but years later the seed she planted blossomed. As a mother teaching her most precious child, I finally completely understood the importance and necessity of differentiated instruction.

Ricky II and I would spend forty-five minutes a day doing this high-energy kinesthetic tactile activity—just touching and feeling and jumping and playing and learning. While doing this, I was able to take notes, and I saw that my son's issues weren't cognitive. He could learn presented information. However, there was definitely a language delay. With my notes in hand, we went back to the doctor's office. After looking at my notes, the doctor agreed: We needed a referral to a speech therapist.

I had just served as Ricky II's advocate for the very first

time. This was amazing—absolutely, positively amazing. As his mom and his teacher, I had taught my son. I had watched my son. I had taken notes and made records. I had gone to the service provider, and something had been done. I was feeling on top of the world. Nothing was going to happen to my little one. Not on my watch.

THE BIRTH OF A SOLUTION

BY AUGUST OF 2008, my husband had been gone about three or four months. Everything was going great with Ricky II and me. I'd found a love for walking, so I walked every day with him, pointing out the components of our environment.

"Look at the tree, Ricky II. Let's feel the leaf. Oh, wow. It's smooth and green and pointy at the tip. This is bark. It's brown and rough. Do you feel that on your hand? That's rough, huh?" I narrated every aspect of our daily life. I was one talking mama.

I found a play group on base that I enjoyed, and I'd met a great group of military wives. Life was just really moving right along. Ricky II was showing progress. The undivided attention I was giving him each day was paying off. He was growing and developing, and he'd actually begun saying more words. He was not yet pairing words together to communicate meaning, but he was pointing and calling out: "Lion, tree, truck, Bono (our dog), bird, cow, fish." I was happy as a pig in mud.

One day, my friend Girlie was visiting our house and watched me engaging in my learning activities with Ricky II. I affectionately called our uninterrupted learning sessions Ricky II Time. It had become our special time together each day. We were on the floor, learning, playing, jumping, rolling around, and making connections—completely in the moment. Ricky II was laughing. I was filling his love bucket, and he was filling mine. We were in our own little world.

After Ricky II and I were finished, Girlie said, "You are using all that energy on one child. You should teach a class."

At first, I thought that was funny. Teach a class? Why would I teach a class about spending time with your child?

Then a little less than a week after Girlie's comment, Ricky II and I were outside, using the playground equipment I had recently purchased to reinforce his gross motor development. We had trampolines, sliding boards, teeter totters, balance beams—anything you could think of, I had it. I had noticed, on the playground, Ricky II wouldn't make any attempts to jump off the play structures like the other kids his age. I got a little concerned. I brought him home and had him stand on a laundry basket and said, "Sweetie, jump." He held my hand and stepped down, but he wouldn't jump. Then I took an aerobic step and asked him to jump down. He wouldn't jump, but, again, he held my hand and stepped down. Finally, I placed a phone book on the floor, had him stand on it and said, "Jump, Baby." He wouldn't jump. I held his hand, and he walked down.

I decided I needed to build confidence in my son. I researched gymnastics and tumbling activities for kids. I enrolled Ricky II in a local gym for gymnastics and purchased equipment for him to use at home. Ricky II and I would have little gross motor skill classes right in our yard as part of our routine.

A neighbor who lived across the street saw us and said, "I used to be a Family Child Care provider," which meant that she used to care for children in a home daycare setting. She continued, "You really should teach a class. You're out here every day working with your son. I think you would do well."

At that point, I realized my neighbor and my friend might be right. Maybe I could teach a class. I decided the next time I took Ricky II to hourly care, I would go to the Child Youth and School Services office on our military installation, introduce myself, and let them know I was interested in teaching a class. I proposed teaching a class for moms and their little ones in my home. But I quickly learned due to the military installation's housing regulation, I would not be able to teach a class in my home. However, I was presented with an interesting counter to my proposal. The US Army had a new program, Skies Unlimited. The objective of the program was to provide military families with child enrichment activities on post. I would serve as an Army contractor, and my classes would be presented to the families of our military community.

I went home and wrote down all the things I did with Ricky II on a daily basis, formatted the activities in a series of forty-five minute classes—and KinderJam was born. With a husband in Iraq and a recent miscarriage I was still trying to process, KinderJam was a welcomed distraction.

KinderJam allowed me to focus all of my energy on my son while simultaneously building a program. Each night at 7:30 I would put my son to bed, and then I would write down all the things we had done that day, all the songs we'd sung, all the activities we'd participated in. I started to build a curriculum for KinderJam.

Now, I had never taught outside of the traditional classroom setting, so this was an adventure for me. How was I going to establish a program in my community using simply the tools I used with my own son, without the backing of an administrator or a school district? It was just me. I would need materials, so I wrote down all the materials I used in the house with Ricky II. From the list, I determined which instructional aids I would use in my new classes. I copied, pasted, drew, hot glued, sewed, and cut until the wee hours of the morning.

I wanted to include music in my class because music was such a large part of the way I was able to communicate with my son. I had a six-disc CD changer, one of those antiquated, old-fashioned disc changers from way back before MP3 players were popular, so that's what I used. I needed a way to transport this large piece of equipment. Ricky II no longer needed his changing table, so I went to Home Depot and purchased a bottle of Gorilla Glue and glued caster wheels to the bottom of the table to make a cart. I put my CD player, my bean bags, pompoms, egg shakers, everything I needed on the table, loaded it in my truck, and drove to the CYSS office to teach KinderJam.

When I first started teaching the classes, they were attended by my son, myself, and my friends and their kids. I would walk all over the base handing out flyers. Then the word began to spread. The FCC providers in the area started attending my class, bringing with them their own children and the four or five other children they cared for in their home daycares. Within months the KinderJam classes were booming.

KinderJam allowed me to share with other parents what I was doing at home with my son. It also allowed me to observe several children that were my son's age so I could have a frame of reference to gauge his progress. But I was not the only one benefiting. KinderJam gave the community a place for parents on base to meet, and it encouraged parents to keep eyes and ears on their children's growth and development. So KinderJam not only became a new career for me, but it became a service for my son and other families with young children in my community. It was my baby. I had lost a child and given birth to an idea that helped my son and other children.

Our First Conversation

IN ADDITION TO my work with KinderJam, I was still working with my son at home, helping him with speech and language. He was also receiving speech and language services at a private agency, and I had taken the information they had given me, along with other material I had purchased from different websites, and had developed a personalized speech and language curriculum for my son.

My husband returned from Iraq to find more than a few new developments. His son was receiving speech and language services, and I was expressing concerns of additional developmental delays I was noticing. His wife had started an Early Childhood Education Enrichment company during his deployment. And we were still a family of three—no new baby.

I also enrolled Ricky II at the Child Development Center on base so he could get more socialization. I volunteered at the center to help create an environment that would be best for my son's success. When my efforts were met with resistance from the Child Development Center's trainer, I sought out a preschool with a culture that would best meet Ricky II's diverse learning needs. My husband was away on a short-term assignment when I told him about my idea for changing preschools.

He felt I was overreacting, but I was beginning to get more comfortable making decisions about Ricky II without my husband, because although he was no longer deployed, he was gone on short travel assignments several times a month and was generally unavailable to me when he was away. I knew in my heart that he didn't have enough face time with Ricky II to accurately assess his progress.

After spending a week visiting and observing preschools in the area, I decided to remove Ricky II from the Child Development Center and enroll him in Teddy Bear Preschool. It was a small, intimate preschool environment with seasoned teachers who were accustomed to working with children with diverse learning needs. I was determined to provide my son with every opportunity for success.

At three years old, Ricky II was now comfortably settled into a wonderful preschool. However, I still felt that need to be near him. I would teach my KinderJam classes and then go to his preschool and spend time with him in the sandbox— his favorite place to be—and have conversations with him and the children. Despite the speech curriculum I had developed, Ricky II still wasn't doing much talking. He had learned some scripted phrases from my husband and me, and he used those at times, but he wasn't having any dialogue or conversation.

On this particular day in the enclosed sandbox, one of the little girls playing in the sandbox said, "Hi, Ricky II's mom. Why doesn't Ricky II ever talk?"

I said, "Oh, well, Ricky II's more of a thinker than a talker. He's a man of little words."

She seemed to be satisfied with my answer, and continued to play. I talked to Ricky II and his friends and narrated to Ricky II the things he was doing. I had a meeting to attend, so I kissed my son and told him bye. I wasn't expecting him to respond, but as I was exiting the sandbox, I heard:

"Bye, mommy."

To this day, I cannot adequately put into words the emotions I felt when my three-year-old said those two words to me that day. He had said the words before, but the difference this time was the way he said it. He meant for his words to reach me, from his mind and his heart through his lips to my ears and straight to my heart. I knew in that moment my baby was going to be okay. We had had our first conversation.

After that, I got a surge of motivation and energy. I felt like a turbo mommy and decided I was going to make sure I took this "Bye, mommy" and just build on it. I knew now that Ricky II could formulate a thought, process it, and then articulate it to me.

I started to look at everything from a different perspective. My son had something inside of his head, and he wanted to get it out. It was my job to help him. I started to look at his speech therapist differently. When Ricky II first started speech therapy, he was about two-and-a-half years old. His speech therapist at the time would watch him play and build her lessons around the toys he chose to play with. But now we were going to a different speech therapist because the first one had been assigned a different case.

I noticed there was a conflict developing between Ricky II and the new therapist. The therapist did not seem to take into consideration that Ricky was only three years old. He had the inclinations of a three-year-old child—to play and move about as opposed to sitting in a seat and looking at flash cards.

The speech therapist wanted Ricky to sit in a chair and focus on prescribed assignments. I felt my child's time was being wasted. He had thirty minutes in his session, and I needed the amount of instruction he was receiving and his opportunities to learn to be maximized.

I didn't discontinue Ricky's speech therapy, but I did take matters into my own hands. By this time, I was going back to school to get a master's in Early Childhood Education. I felt I needed to be as capable as the people who were instructing my son so if there were any gaps, I could fill them in. One of the things I learned from being a teacher and working with professionals was the amount of variables that could come into the classroom. Teachers are people. Service providers are people. They have family situations. They have job situations. Sometimes they're late to work. They have kids of their own that they may be concerned about. Although they might be quality service providers, they weren't going to be nearly as invested in my child's success as I was as his parent and as his primary educator.

I felt confident about the information I was learning in graduate school, and I applied all of my research to my son. My evaluations were indicating that speech and language were not the only issues in his development. But I stayed the course. Then one day, while I was in the waiting room during Ricky's appointment with his new therapist, I realized I was really uncomfortable with the setup of the office. At the former office, each room had glass windows. I could see and hear the session without being in the room. This particular office was smaller, and I was asked to wait in the waiting room while the speech therapist worked with my three-year-old in a private room, with the door closed and no window.

On one particular day, while sitting in the waiting room, I heard my child scream.

I got up.

Another scream.

I couldn't get to the door fast enough.

As the third scream came out his mouth, I opened the door. "What's wrong, Baby?" An attendant told me parents must remain in the waiting area. I ignored her. "Are you okay, Baby?" He looked at me. He had no words.

The speech therapist said to me, "He's okay. I would hope that you would trust me."

"Trust you? I don't know you. This is my child, and he is in distress. If you insist on a closed-door policy, it's time for me to take my baby and leave."

And that was exactly what I did.

After my inner Mama Bear had growled and settled down, I realized my baby would now need me to find another new speech therapist—and pronto. I reached out to a friend, who was an Educational Psychologist for the local school district, to see if she could expedite an IEP process to get Ricky II services through the school system before the end of the school year. An IEP, Individualized Education Program, is the legal document that defines a child's special education program. An IEP includes the reason under which a child qualifies for Special Education Services, the services the IEP team has determined the school will provide, yearly goals and objectives, and any accommodations that must be made to assist a child in learning. Ricky II was not yet school aged, but I knew from my days in the classroom that if I got him on an IEP, even at three years old, he could receive services from the local elementary school as long as I provided transportation. My friend was able to expedite the process, and we were successful in getting Ricky assessed and deemed eligible for an IEP.

I wanted to get him in before the end of the school year so I could get material to work with him through the summer months. We were extremely fortunate. The speech therapist assigned to us was amazing! She worked so well with Ricky II and allowed me to stay in the room during their sessions. I learned many strategies from her to help my son, but the most important thing she did for us was say the words "Autism Spectrum" out loud. It was a blow and a relief at the same time to hear those words.

I had a gnawing feeling and had done some studying on my own and knew that Ricky II had some of the characteristics of Autism Spectrum Disorder. I told my husband what the speech therapist said and what I felt. He was not ready to receive this information, understandably.

I went into high gear and read everything I could get my hands on about autism. I told Ricky II's pediatrician, who still wasn't seeing what I was seeing because Ricky II was a healthy, engaging, and responsive toddler. But I knew that for the amount of input I was giving my son, there should have been more of an output.

One day while out shopping at the mall, my soul just felt tired. I didn't know what to do. I had gotten him speech therapy services. I'd had him evaluated. He had an IEP. I knew he was capable of more than what was being produced. I just didn't have the key to unlock it. I needed someone to tell me what to do.

I walked out of the store, got in my truck, and called up Miss Raejeana. By this time, her son Shannon was a college student. She had managed to create successful opportunities for him. There were so many things about Ricky II at this young age that reminded me of my time spent with Shannon and Miss Raejeana. I called her and said, "Miss Raejeana, I need to help my baby. Please tell me what to do."

She calmed me down and said, "Listen. You are Mama Bear. You can get him all the help and assistance that he needs. Now, this is what we're going to do. I want you to call your nearest teaching hospital, and I want you to talk to the behavioral science department in the children's hospital and tell them what you just told me. I went through the same thing with Shannon. You are Mama Bear. You follow your gut. I don't care if everyone tells you he's okay. I don't care if everyone tells you that it's just fine. That baby doesn't have time for you to wait this out. If your gut is telling you different, act on it."

When I got off the phone with Miss Raejeana, I took out my iPad and researched Stanford University's Children's Hospital behavioral science department. In the parking lot of Macy's, I called.

Through my tears, I said, "Hello. My name is El Brown, and I need help for my son, Ricky II. I know something is going on with him. For the amount of input I am giving him, there should be more of an output. I need someone to put eyes on my baby."

"Ma'am, slow down. Let's start from the beginning so we can get your son the help that he needs."

I took a deep breath. Someone was going to listen to me.

They asked me some specific questions about Ricky II's situation, and I was able to give them answers based on the notes I had taken. I was then instructed to go to my pediatrician and tell him what I had just told them and ask for a referral to Lucile Packard Children's Hospital Stanford. My husband and I did just that. We made an appointment for the very next day, and I was given a referral to Stanford University.

Along with the referral came a lot of paperwork, checklists I had to fill out, evaluations I had to complete. Additionally his preschool, service providers, and doctor had to complete a series of forms as well. I was diligent about all of it. I made sure everyone got everything done in a timely manner so I could get this back to Stanford as soon as possible.

Then I got a call from Ricky II's doctor's office informing us that the paperwork was ready. As soon as I picked up the paperwork, I made sure to review everything in the car before I left, just in case there was something I didn't agree with. Then I saw it…

AUTISM. MODERATE.

I HAD NEVER seen the word "autism" next to my son's name. As I said before, I'd had my own suspicions and done my own research. I had noticed his spinning, his lack of eye contact. He used echolalia, or repetition, to communicate. I knew there were some symptoms there that were indicative of a child on the spectrum. However, with all the service providers and all the doctor visits, no one but the speech therapist had ever said it. Now, because I had pushed the issue, I was seeing the words in print for the first time. My heart hurt for my child. But I was going to make sure that he was going to be okay—better than okay. Ricky II was going to be SUPER!

I introduced the concept of "Super Kid" to Ricky and began to ingrain in him that he was a Super Kid. I worked to teach him all the rote skills he could absorb, because higher-order thinking was a challenge for him. At four years old, he was not yet talking beyond two-to-three–word phrases. However, he could grasp rote skills rather quickly thanks to his echolalia, which enabled him to parrot very clearly what he heard. After enough repetition, I noticed he would retain most of the information introduced to him.

Months later, we prepared to travel to our appointment

at Stanford University. We decided to make a weekend of it, a family vacation. We didn't want the assessment to be the focal point of the weekend. It was going to be a six-hour process. Regardless of the outcome, we were determined to make it a weekend about enjoying our perfectly formed Super Kid.

On Friday, February 18, 2011, the day of the assessment, Ricky II saw a series of specialists. He was a trooper that day, and after a six-hour behavioral assessment, the doctor came into the office and gave her official diagnosis: Autism Spectrum Disorder (ASD).

My breath was taken away for two reasons. I hurt for my child because I did not understand why he was chosen to face this obstacle. I was also relieved. I was relieved to know I wasn't crazy. I was relieved to know that now we had a name, and now we could get assistance and work toward creating every successful opportunity for Ricky II to maximize his potential.

Although we now had a diagnosis, a name—Autism—nothing changed for me. He had walked into that hospital as Ricky II and come out as Ricky II. And I had walked into that hospital as his mother and walked out still his mother.

BUILDING A VILLAGE

I BELIEVE IN the importance of a village, a tribe of close friends, and I knew I could not make this journey on my own. So I reached out to my circle of mothers and sister-friends.

From: El Brown
Sent: Sunday, February 20, 2011 7:09 AM
To: undisclosed recipients
Subject: Leaning on your friendship

Hello Sister Friends,

If you are receiving this email, it is because you have touched my life in a significant way and I value you as a mother, a woman, and a friend. Anyone who knows me knows that my heart and all I do in this world revolve around the love of my life, my son, Ricky II. Since the time of his conception, I have prayed over his little soul and vowed to love him and give him every opportunity for success. Ricky II has been and will always be my miracle child. Pregnancies have not been an easy road for me. Ricky II was a twin, and as the little fighter he is, he held on so he could make it to his momma's loving arms. I have had two miscarriages since Ricky II's birth and have come to terms with the fact that Ricky II may be my only child. I am okay with that; he is my world and a child perfectly designed for me.

Friday, my husband and I took Ricky II to Stanford Children's Hospital. I have known Ricky II had some developmental delays for some time now. We started out with Speech and Language assistance, and as a mother, I knew there was something more. About four months ago, I reached out to Stanford, and they told me the procedures to follow to get my local doctors to act on my concerns. On Friday, February 18, 2011, the love of my life was diagnosed with autism. My heart is broken for him right now. I am questioning why my little man was chosen to overcome this obstacle. But through my tears, I know I need to be strong because I am his mother. So with that, I come to each of you. I know I get busy and life prevents me from reaching out as much as my heart would like me to. However, I am smart enough to know this is not a road I can travel successfully without sistahfriends and prayer warriors. I am in so much pain right now, it is difficult to breathe. Life has given me many tests, and I have endured them all. But to watch my child's strength tested is more than my heart can endure right now. So I am reaching out to each of you and asking for your prayers, concern, and to borrow some of your strength because I am so weak and hurt right now.

Love,
El

SHARPENING OUR SKILLS

I KNEW THERE was a long road ahead of us, but I also knew we could travel it. It was going to require work, but now that we had a diagnosis, I was going to be able to build a Super Team to help our Super Kid.

By California standards, Ricky II was eligible to start kindergarten in the fall, but I knew he wasn't ready to be a school-aged child yet. He had a late birthday and a new diagnosis. I did something that might be considered a little unorthodox. Because of staffing issues and the frequent turnaround in the school district's service providers, I had lost faith in the school system's ability to assist Ricky's development in the manner in which I knew he required. Ricky was four years old, and we had no time to waste. I believe that it is a parent's prerogative to work for their child's best interests. If you have the resources, use them. If you don't, find them.

I was a stay-at-home mom, so therefore I had an unlimited amount of time to work with my son. I was also an educator by trade, so I had years of experience working with small children. By that time, I was partway through a master's program for early childhood education, and I was taking classes, workshops, and seminars, all to better myself to be able to provide

Ricky II with everything he needed. I honestly felt, at that particular time in our lives, that I was in a position to implement a personal IEP.

I chose to take a more behavioral approach to Ricky II's development. We enlisted the service of a licensed clinical social worker and started Floortime with Ricky II. Floortime is a therapeutic approach developed by the late Dr. Stanley Greenspan. Floortime meets children where they are and builds upon their strengths and abilities through interacting and creating a warm relationship. The approach challenges children to go further and to develop who they are rather than what their diagnosis says they are.

During Floortime, we connected with Ricky II and his interests and challenged him to be creative, curious, and spontaneous in an effort to move him forward intellectually and emotionally. I learned to follow Ricky II's lead, how to step into his world and teach from the inside out. I learned to encourage his creativity and spontaneity and to work with him purposefully while including all his senses, motor skills, and emotions.

Floortime was a game changer for me and for Ricky II. Through Floortime, we set goals for his development. And we saw tremendous progress.

ESTABLISHING A SCHOOL ENVIRONMENT

I WAS ENDING my master's degree program, and I needed a school site to complete my practicum. I went into an Early Childhood Education environment and became an apprentice for a while. I wanted to use my practicum time to further research school environments that would be best suited for Ricky II.

I had been introduced to the Reggio Emilia approach to learning during my studies. I understood it to be a completely child-centered environment, and I understood the academic portion of a Reggio Emilia curriculum. However, I did not know what it looked like in the context of real life because my background was elementary education. There's a huge difference between elementary education and early childhood education and child development. We are very process-oriented in early childhood education. We are concerned with the process that a child goes through to learn all the things they need in order to be lifelong learners.

While watching the teachers at the Monterey Peninsula College Child Development Center, where I chose to do my practicum, I thought, *Wow. This is the type of program that*

Ricky II needs to be a part of. This was the program where they had professionally trained educators to foster the learning of the children. One of the core beliefs of this particular school, which had the Reggio Emilia–inspired curriculum, was that children know what they need to learn. Our job as educators is to support this learning. This approach to learning fit hand-in-hand with the Floortime strategies we were using with Ricky II.

I sat in on one of their staff meetings. They were planning for the next school year. One of the teachers said, "We're going to have centers throughout the outside area for their outdoor exploration. We're going to take out the blocks and the equipment for the dramatic play area, and we'll take out the tools for the gardening area."

Another teacher said, "I don't think that's a good idea. If we bring out blocks, then the students will feel as though they have to do whatever they need to do that day to learn with those blocks."

The other teacher responded and said, "Are you saying we should just open the cabinets and say, 'What do you want to learn today?'"

"Exactly. As teachers, it is our job to know the standards. Therefore, instead of walking into a room and saying, 'These are the standards we are going to learn today. Follow me,' we should look at our little ones and watch what they are experiencing today and find the standards in that."

As a parent, I thought, *BOOM! YES! I love him!*

Essentially he was saying instead of walking into a room and saying, "Today we're going to work on the color green. This is the color green. This is a green crayon. This is a piece of paper. Can you draw a green apple? Can you draw a green leaf?" he was saying, "Let's go outside and watch our children explore their environment. When they pick up a leaf, say, 'Oh, that's a nice leaf. It feels very smooth, and it's such a beautiful green color.' We are teaching the children in the context of their real life experience."

That is what I had been doing for Ricky II since his birth. I then knew that this was the school my son needed to attend.

As much as I knew this new environment would be beneficial for Ricky II's developmental needs, changing schools was an extremely difficult decision for me. My son was part of a preschool environment that I loved—I mean really LOVED. The teachers at Teddy Bear Preschool were more like aunties to my son than teachers. My family was military, and we lived far away from other family. When I would take my child to Teddy Bear Preschool, I felt as though I was taking him to a family's home, to our family's home. The teachers there were very loving. They nurtured Ricky II. They cared for Ricky II. When I initially took him to Teddy Bear Preschool, that's what he needed. That's what I needed.

Now I was realizing that Ricky II was four years old and it was time for him to graduate to a different type of school environment. I learned a very important lesson about being Ricky II's mom through this experience. I had grown so attached to Teddy Bear Preschool and so attached to the loving and nurturing environment that he received there, that there was a little part of my heart that wanted him to stay there forever. It can be difficult to let go of what you know works and what you feel most comfortable with. It was difficult for me to place my child in the position to be challenged differently, but I had to if I wanted him to continue to grow and increase his exposure and capabilities.

I talked to the teachers at Teddy Bear and the teachers at the Monterey Peninsula College Child Development Center, and they helped me understand that I was creating a village for Ricky II. He would always have the loving experiences he'd had at Teddy Bear to lean on as a foundation, and I would always have the relationship I'd built with the teachers at Teddy Bear to rely on. Now he was graduating to a new experience, and that was just a part of growing up, a part of childhood and a part of development. He was going to a larger school with different teachers, a different transition, and that would prepare him for future transitions.

We made the switch. I will admit it was difficult for me for the first week, maybe two, because I was very accustomed to Teddy Bear's way of doing things with Ricky II. I was more reluctant than he was about the change, even though the change was my idea.

In the spirit of creating a village, before Ricky II went for his first day at his new school, we brought in our licensed clinical social worker. She provided an in-service to the teachers so they could better understand what autism looked like for Ricky II. It was important for me as a parent to make this distinction. Many people have an idea of what autism looks like, but autism is a spectrum. If you've met one child on the spectrum, you've only met one child on the spectrum. No two children with autism are exactly the same.

Now that Ricky II was going to be part of a new environment, we wanted to show the teachers in that environment what he was like. How does Ricky II relate to adults? How does he relate to children? That in-service was one of the greatest experiences of my personal and professional life. I sat in that in-service with those teachers and watched them ask questions of the licensed clinical social worker so they could be better prepared to meet Ricky II's specific needs once he entered their school.

After we settled in, Ricky II's new school environment was a wonderful experience. I watched him grow and develop in ways that I didn't think would be possible so early on. I watched him make new friends. I watched him engage in conversation with other children. I even watched him move beyond parallel play to actually interact with other kids in give-and-take situations. I was very optimistic about his growth and development during his time at the Monterey Peninsula College Child Development Center.

However, we were a military family, which meant every location was temporary. We had finally gotten into a rhythm of making it work, to a point where Ricky II was moving and progressing quickly. We had a licensed clinical therapist we loved. Ricky II had graduated from Floortime to group therapy. He was in a buddy group where he met with other children who had processing issues they were working on. Group therapy was hosted by physical therapists and social workers who facilitated play. He was making friends, and life was good for him. And life was great for us as his parents because our joy came from watching him grow and develop.

Now faced with an upcoming move, my husband asked me, "If we could go anywhere in the world, where would you like to go?" I immediately said the Washington DC area, specifically Fairfax County. I was familiar with the school system in Fairfax County because I was recruited to work there right out of college and had worked with several teachers from the FCPS system when I taught overseas with the Department of Defense Education Activity (DoDEA). FCPS was progressive and resource-friendly. The schools were staffed to have full classroom inclusion, so Ricky II would be able to get all of his services right on his school site.

I was confident in my ability to advocate for my son, but I had learned from the current location's school district that you can't advocate for a district to give your child resources they don't have. I feared if we were relocated to a smaller, less resource-friendly area, the type of assistance Ricky II required to continue his current rate of progress might not be available in the public school environment.

Secondly, I was teaching Ricky II that he was a Super Kid. So I needed him to live in an area that was progressive, diverse, and forward-thinking enough to embrace his differences, reinforce what I had been teaching, and give him the opportunity to develop into his greatness without dampening his self-esteem.

We enrolled Ricky II in the military's Exceptional Family Member Program (EFMP) to increase our likelihood of receiving orders to the DC area. We were successful. After receiving official orders to report to DC, my husband and I sat down together and devised a plan about what we were going to do to ensure that Ricky II continued to thrive, because we didn't want any lapses in progress due to a move. I started to research schools and programs in autism. I researched test scores, demographics, everything you could think of via Greatschools.org. I polled parents. We finally narrowed our search down to a specific area within Fairfax, Virginia.

Now we needed to determine which school. This move would be completely different from any move we'd made before. This would be our first time moving with a school-aged child. My husband and I agreed that we needed to let the school dictate where we would stay within the DC Metro area.

By the grace of God, we found a wonderful elementary school. From California, I called several local schools. I would introduce myself and explain that I had a rising kindergartener who was on the autism spectrum. At one elementary school, the most pleasant school secretary answered. Her voice and demeanor immediately put me at ease. After I explained my reason for calling, she responded by saying, "Oh, we would be so happy to have Ricky II. Let me transfer you to the special education department." Her words made my heart smile. The school secretary transferred me to the special education chairperson, who wasn't available, so I left her a message.

I don't know if I was really expecting her to give me a call back, but she did. She happened to call while I was teaching a KinderJam class, so I missed the call. I called her back, and once again, she wasn't in, so I left another message. This time, I gave her my husband's number because he was always in his office. She called my husband repeatedly until she got him. Mind you, there is a three-hour time difference between California and Virginia, so she called him after school hours on her personal time to ensure that she got him. Our question as parents was, "What would you need from us to ensure that our son has the easiest, if possible, seamless transition into kindergarten next year?" We were advised to go back to the school district in Monterey and get an IEP update. With a month left, we went through all of the necessary assessments and evaluations.

We came to DC a month later with an updated IEP and brought it to the school. We were extremely comfortable with this school at this point, so we signed on a home that was within walking distance of the school.

By this time, there were only thirty days left in the school year. I discussed with my husband the possibility of enrolling Ricky II in kindergarten to go ahead and finish out the year so he could learn the school, teachers, routine, and get used to his new environment. He needed to learn to work on a schedule and to experience PE and recess because these things were not part of preschool. I wanted him to become familiar with his new school environment so when he started in the fall, he could hit the ground running.

We took this idea to the special education chairman, and she thought it was a wonderful idea. We enrolled our baby into kindergarten with thirty days left. Now, I had no idea how this would fare or if I was making the right decision. I just knew that he'd just made this move across the country, and if I could give him the opportunity to see what his next year would look like, we could possibly eliminate some of the social transitions and focus on the academic skills that kindergarten had to offer in the fall.

Much to our pleasure, Ricky II took to elementary school like a fish to water. I would walk him to school every day. He loved taking his lunch and eating snacks in the classroom. He loved his teachers. He loved making new friends. And in his own words, walking to school one day, he said, "I love elementary school. I love kindergarten." I was so proud of him. I was so proud of our journey.

Ricky II would come home every day and tell us about all the things he had learned in class. We were blessed to have teachers who communicated with us daily to let us know his progress. I couldn't have been happier. And when the school year was coming to a close, I had to explain to Ricky II that although kindergarten would soon be coming to an end, it would start again in the fall. My baby looked up at me and said, "Mommy, I love school." At that moment, everything I had worked for as his mother from the time I was 18 years old to this moment with my son was worth it.

We had managed to instill an enthusiasm about learning. We had sheltered his self-esteem. We nurtured his confidence. We provided opportunity for his growth and development. Our son loved school. The icing on the cake was the day Ricky II came home with a Student Achievement Award, which was a little dog tag they put around his neck and a little certificate they gave him. When I went to pick him up that day, the principal and teachers told me about the award. But more importantly, Ricky II told me about the award. He was so pleased with himself, and I was so happy.

It didn't stop there. At the end of that year of kindergarten, our baby received the Good Listener Award. Everything that I had done came to this moment where my son stood before me with eyes beaming, so proud of his efforts, so proud of his successes. My journey to create successful opportunities for my son was just beginning, but a foundation had been laid within my son, within our family, and within myself. I am proud to say I am my child's first educator and greatest advocate. I am Mama Bear.

PART II
MEET SDK

BY JUNE OF 2012, I had successfully guided my little guy to kindergarten with lots of prayer, patience, and hard work. Much of our time was spent with me inputting information into his little mind and spirit, hoping and praying it would begin to gel together at some point. Well, by the grace of God, it did! Soon after his brief time in kindergarten, I began to see the emergence of this funny, clever, and charismatic little person. It seemed all the things I had taught him over the last five years were coming together all at once. I couldn't keep all of this goodness to myself. So, I took to social media. I began to journal about Ricky II and my feelings as his mother on Facebook and Instagram because I wanted to encourage parents. I wanted them to know that while the gratification of their efforts might be delayed, the seeds they were planting in their child would harvest in time. So I decided to give families a peek inside the life of a child living with autism.

Now, I understand that every child is different and Ricky II's story is his own. However, it was my prayer that some

parent or teacher could find a bit of their child or student in my journaling of life with Ricky II and know that we are all in this journey together. And I have the same prayer for you. The journal that follows picks up where my story ends and my little guy's story begins. I had the blessing of watching him become a little person who was beginning to discover his place in the world. I shared this process and my insight and emotions as a spectator to this wonderful occurrence though journaling. While reading entries from my journal, you will witness the real-life, daily experience of a Mama Bear meeting and celebrating her cub. I pray SDK (SuperDuperKid) inspires you as he has inspired me.

FIVE YEARS OLD

June 15, 2012

I thank God for wonderful, competent, compassionate, and enthusiastic teachers. Ricky II has been blessed with four of them. They have made our transition to Fairfax seamless. I am able to go out and conquer the world every day because my mind is free because I know my baby is well cared for. Great teachers are one of a family's greatest blessings. Thank a teacher today! #Grateful

June 17, 2012

Six weeks without my baby… I've got to find a project to keep me busy. I guess it's time to write and publish my first book.

June 17, 2012

Ricky II and Pete the Cat are ready to roll! Can you tell someone is just a little happy to be spending the summer with Grandma and Grandpa!

June 20, 2012

Ricky II is away for the summer. Big Ricky has 5 days off for the 4th of July Weekend. Guess what we're going to do: A) take a weekend cruise and watch the sunset behind the ocean as we gaze into each other's eyes, arms intertwined, sipping on champagne, B) have a relaxing staycation in the Nation's Capital, dinner and dancing followed by a horse-drawn carriage ride and a stay in a luxury hotel, or C) fly down to Florida to see our little man and take him to LEGOLAND® Florida, fight the summer tourist crowds, waiting in long lines while enduring the Florida sun? #WeLoveBeingHisParents

June 24, 2012

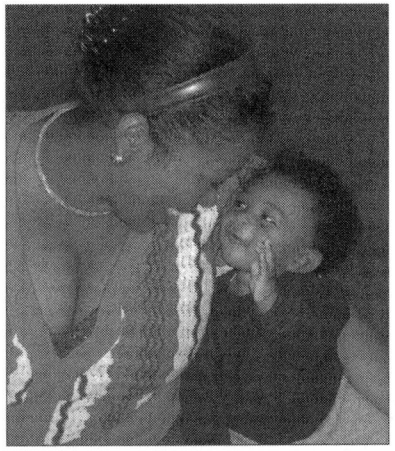

My favorite picture of Ricky II and me. From day one he has always known he could tell his mommy anything and she would listen.

June 24, 2012

Ricky II is NOT missing us! Grandpa made a rope swing!

June 24, 2012

Nope, not missing the parents!

June 24, 2012

My child just kicked us off the phone. "Okay, bye, Mommy, bye, Daddy!" He swears he has business and things to do! He is enjoying his summer! #BLESSED!

July 3, 2012

Going to see our little man! Feels like Christmas!

July 3, 2012

I got my baby!

July 26, 2012

I'm realizing my life isn't nearly as interesting when Ricky II is away. He is the color in my days. Sixteen-day countdown…

July 27, 2012

Can you tell I'm just a little bit excited about my baby coming home? Kindergarten Workstation is complete. All that is missing is my Ricky II! #15DayCountDown

July 27, 2012

My baby said in his nightly prayers, "Thank you, Jesus, for my hair cut today and helping me keep still." #ILoveThatLittleBoy #MamaDon'tPlayBoutThemHairCuts

August 5, 2012

This time next week, my baby will be home! Woot! Woot!

August 12, 2012

I got my baby back! All is right in the world. #ILoveHim #Family

August 12, 2012

After eight weeks of having a child-free home, I walked in the kitchen and saw a little pair of black Nikes in the middle of the floor and some little white socks and a deflated balloon in the middle of the family room floor. Instead of fussing, I just smiled. My baby is home and marking his territory.

August 13, 2012

Okay, the honeymoon is over. How did I forget how much work it was to entertain an energetic 5-year-old boy?! It's not even 9:30 and we are on our seventh activity of the day. AND he found a noise maker in his room. Man, I should have thrown that thing out while he was gone. #RealWorld

August 16, 2012

Nineteen days before the first day of school, and I am already having anxiety and nightmares about my baby's first year of big-boy school… Jesus be a Xanax.

August 16, 2012

I just asked Ricky II if he wanted a grilled cheese sandwich, and he said, "Yes, please, but with the white, round cheese." Did he just request Provolone cheese?!
#HeIsTooMuch #MomTheShortOrderCook

August 29, 2012

He is so proud of himself. He went to his room, chose his clothes from his closet, and dressed himself from head to toe with no assistance from Mommy! #MyBigBoy

August 30, 2012

Open House at Ricky II's school today. Kindergarten starts next Tuesday. Thirteen years 'til a high school graduation with honors. #LetsGetIt

September 4, 2012

First Day of Kindergarten!!!

September 9, 2012

Today Ricky II worshipped with us in the main sanctuary, and the senior choir sang. Ricky II pointed at the choir and said, "Look at all the grandmas! Where's Hyacinth Brown?" I think it's time for Grandma to come for a visit!

September 12, 2012

Still amazed at the fact that the tiny baby we brought home from the hospital is in Kindergarten. #InAwe

September 15, 2012

Ricky II's 6th birthday: Under the Big Top!

SIX YEARS OLD

September 17, 2012

Okay, so the five of us are walking home from school: me, Ricky II, and his three imaginary friends, Gingerbread Boy, Black Clover, and Elmo. Ordinarily, I would not have a problem letting his friends walk home with us, but today I'm having to stop every thirty seconds because Ricky II keeps telling me that Gingerbread Boy, Black Clover, and Elmo are playing in the street. Umm, I'm gonna need their imaginary mama to come get them and teach them some home training. I got my hands full with my one.

September 20, 2012

Our Birthday Boy! Happy 6th Birthday, Ricky II! Mommy and Daddy love you so much!

September 26, 2012

Today our Little Big Boy requested that I just walk him to the front of the school and let him walk in the school and to his classroom by himself. I respected his wishes... kind of. Imagine me doing my best Pink Panther impression, tiptoeing a safe distance behind him, peeping around corners, and peering through cracks in the door. #YeahImTHATMama

September 28, 2012

Going to the circus tonight, and Ricky II is wearing his ringmaster costume from his birthday party. I gotta get my money's worth! #CostPerWear

September 28, 2012

Apparently, today is Spirit Day at my son's school. I walked him in the door wearing blue and grey and was met by a sea of kids and teachers wearing green and white. Ricky II looked up at me like he was saying, "Umm, I'm gonna need you to do better." Okay… so I ran home and ironed some green and white and brought it back to him. He was so not impressed. #Shamming

September 30, 2012

I know Ricky II is doing something he isn't supposed to be doing in the basement. It's way too quiet down there. But I'm afraid to go down there and look because I have ONE nerve left, and it has to last us the rest of the night, so I'm trying to ration out my stress so that ONE nerve lasts 'til his bedtime.

October 4, 2012

I am 2,000 miles away from home, but my baby is squared away because the Lord blessed me with a mother-in-law who took a cab, a bus, and a train to VA to volunteer in her grandbaby's class, chaperone his first field trip, taxi him to his enrichment classes, and give him warm milk and honey before he goes to bed at night. I am blessed beyond measure. #Family #Grateful

October 14, 2012

I thought because it's Sunday… maybe, just maybe I would get to sleep in 'til at least 8am. But apparently, I have a custom alarm set to "Mommy, my tummy is growling. It's time for breakfast. Get up" at 7am. #EveryDayIsMonday

October 17, 2012

Ricky II has his first Spanish class today after school. Hopefully they can break him of his broken "Dora Spanglish." *¡Vamos! Hola, Boots. ¿Cómo estás? Swiper no Swiping!*

October 18, 2012

Kindergarten is expensive! Every week since Ricky II has been in school I have had to send money in or donate items to his class: Scholastic Book Club, school pictures, weekly reader donation, hand soap, Foreign Language class, school spirit apparel, field trips, PTA fundraisers, monthly teachers' appreciation breakfasts, pasta, Fall Festival... He's in public school now, but I'm going to have to put school expenses back in the budget. #MoneyInMoneyOut

October 31, 2012

Out Trick or Treatin', and my child is not motivated. He is looking at me like, "Can we just go to Target and buy some candy?" #21stCenturyKids

November 7, 2012

I hate that my little man is sick. But I have to admit he is the best little cuddle buddy when he's under the weather. #SnuggleTime

November 7, 2012

He may be home sick, but give me a paper plate and a piece of paper and class is in session! #MyMommyIsATeacher

November 8, 2012

I really have a great kid! How did we get so blessed?

November 8, 2012

Just another day in the life of Ricky II. #Individuality

November 10, 2012

My baby just passed his test and earned his belt! #ProudMama

November 16, 2012

Friday Night at The Browns #3Generations #Family #LoveThem

November 17, 2012

Today I am thankful for great and active grandparents. We are blessed to have grandparents who look at Ricky II with the same eyes that we do. They too see ABSOLUTE PERFECTION when they look at our little man. Although the military keeps us far away, they make several trips a year and stay for extended periods of time to ensure their relationship with Ricky II stays strong. In their 60s, they both still run races, build swings, make kites, and go flying, walk to the park, play Candyland and Hide and Seek, volunteer at his school, go fishing, walk him to school and pick him up, come up from Florida if we need extended child care, and give him hugs, kisses, high fives, encouragement, and love without end. And when they are here, they do laundry, housekeeping, and any other project Big Ricky and I haven't had the time to start or finish. And they do it all with a smile and a heart of joy and love. Thank you so much, Grandma and Grandpa Brown. We thank God for you! #ProfessionalGrandparents

November 18, 2012

The conversation in the back of the car is hilarious. Ricky II is giving Grandpa Brown the "Church Rules." LOL! "Grandpa, no running in church. No loud talking or shouting in church, or we will take you outside. Okay, Grandpa?" #PureComedy

November 19, 2012

It feels so weird going to the commissary and getting a regular cart instead of the Rocket. My baby is in school... #SniffSniff #MissingHim

November 23, 2012

Ricky II, Big Ricky, and Grandpa Brown just left for Home Depot. I will be staying home. Ricky II has informed me that Home Depot is not for moms. *blank stare* #MyChild

November 23, 2012

Today on CNN, I watched the White House Christmas Tree arrive for the First Family and get our FABULOUS First Lady's approval, and this evening I find out The Browns will be attending the White House's Holiday Open House! I'm so excited I could pee in my pants! Ricky II is going to be AMAZED when he sees that tree!

November 23, 2012

Trimming his tree. #3Generations #Family

November 25, 2012

This is Ricky II's interpretation of his favorite sculpture, "The Beckoning" by Albert Paley, located at National Harbor. He did it all by himself from memory. He named his sculpture "Imagination." #OurLittleSculptor #ProudMommy

December 1, 2012

WHEW! Crisis averted! I mistakenly started cutting Ricky II's hair without the guard. Lots of prayer and three haircuts later, I fixed it! Can't have a jacked up head at the White House. A photo with a bad haircut lasts forever. #AdventuresInTheKitchenBarberShop

December 1, 2012

He's getting the Mommy Side Eye. We're about to enter the White House, and I'm going over the expectations for behavior. Ricky II is asking a million "what if" questions. "Oh, No… No… No, Partner. You will not break anything in the Obamas' home… Our pockets don't run that deep."

December 1, 2012

Entering the White House. Let the adventure begin — at The White House.

December 5, 2012

Ricky II just announced that he wants Santa to bring him a tuba! Old Man Nic, don't even THINK about it! #OverMyDeadBody

December 9, 2012

I have reached an all-time parenting low. While reading an *I Spy* book with Ricky II and Jordan, we got stumped looking for the dolphin. After 15+ minutes of searching, Ricky II was still determined to find that dolphin. I told them to go play and I would continue to search the page. I went to Google to find the dolphin, then called up to the boys, "I found it!" Yeah, I took all the credit. They think I'm pretty amazing...

December 11, 2012

OMG! I recently posted a pic of my baby's interpretation of Albert Paley's sculpture, "The Beckoning." Well, a representative of the Paley Studios saw the picture on our KinderJam page! They have posted Ricky II's sculpture on their FB page, printed it out, and hung it on the refrigerator in the studio, and are sending Ricky II a signed copy of Albert Paley's book of his work! I am blown away! #ProudMama #ThankYou #Blessed

December 15, 2012

Ricky II just received a book of Albert Paley's work from the Paley Studios in the mail! It is signed by Mr. Paley, and he wrote a message to Ricky II! Amazing! He LOVES it! Thank you! #WOW #ProudMama

December 17, 2012

Monday morning school attire: rockin' a Tae-Kwon-Do belt and a hoodie. Who am I to mess with his personal sense of style? #Individuality

December 24, 2012

'Twas the Night before Christmas…

December 25, 2012

Christmas Eve = The one night a year that it is not a struggle or a negotiation to get Ricky II to bed. He went down… wanted Big Ricky out of his room… and the lights OFF so Santa could do his thing!!!!

January 29, 2013

When does a trip to the commissary become an all-day endeavor? When your six year old insists on riding in "The Rocket," which holds little to no groceries so you have to make more than one trip inside the commissary to get through your grocery list. The cashier said, "Hey, this is like Déjà vu!" Yeah, not quite the word I was thinking…

February 5, 2013

Report Card Day! Woot! Woot! Proud parents of a Super Kid! #GodIsGood #PraisesToTheMostHigh #HeartBursting

February 9, 2013

Helping Mommy with her late night sweet tooth. The beginning stages of my grandmama's Sour Cream Pound Cake. #LateNightBaking

February 10, 2013

I got a little overconfident while giving Ricky II a haircut this morning and nicked his ear. It started to bleed (just a little bit), and this child looked up at me and said, "Not so hard. Don't cut my ear again. This is not supposed to be surgery." I almost dropped the clippers. I guess he TOLD me. *walks to the time-out chair* #StillStunned

February 11, 2013

I Love Bugs!!! Valentine's Day Love Bugs… #100%Boy

February 14, 2013

I think Ricky II's teacher just told us in an email that we are NOT invited to the class Valentine's Day Party. Big Ricky sent her an email asking what time the party starts. She replied, "I didn't send invitations out to parents as we are trying to keep the party 'low key.'" Ummm, trying to rob us of our photo ops... #WeAreNotAboveCrashing

February 19, 2013

Processing issues, learning differences, special rights, speech and language, or ANY other obstacle the universe can place in front of our children is NO match for a PRAYING, HARDWORKING, and DEDICATED MAMA! We are our babies' single greatest asset! Success is the ONLY option! Cheers to Team Mama Bears! I am so proud of you! #NotOnOurWatch #WootWoot

February 25, 2013

Today, I make a promise to me to never overextend myself again... There is power and peace in the word "No." I value me, my time, my energy, and my family.

February 26, 2013

Parent engagement in schools is defined as parents and school staff working together to support and improve the learning, development, and health of children.
#StartEarly
#PositiveParentEngagement

March 26, 2013

Ricky II's finished Gak! Super easy, science fun!

April 8, 2013

suc·cess (sk-ss)

n

1. The achievement of something desired, planned, or attempted: attributed their success in business to hard work

a. The gaining of fame or prosperity: an artist spoiled by success.

b. The extent of such gain.

2. One that is successful: The plan was a success.

3. Obsolete: A result or an outcome.

[Latin successus, from past participle of succedere, to succeed; see succeed.

fail·ure (fl-yr)

n.

1. Not an option

April 8, 2013

Missing my dear friend Vette today. It's been almost three years since she has been gone from this earth. She is the strongest woman and military spouse I have ever met. I taught her oldest son in Korea, and she just had a glow about her that drew everyone to her. I have patterned much of my life as a mother and a woman after her incredible example. I hear her words in my ear daily, and I know she is rooting for me from beyond. I have an angel. #DivineSisterhood

April 11, 2013

People often say the grass is not always greener on the other side. To that I say, grass is completely overrated anyway. In my travels, I have seen many different types of landscapes. In California, I saw beautiful white rocks and succulent gardens. In Japan, I had black beach sand. In Korea, I had cement lined with fruit trees. In the Southwest, I saw beautiful red and orange sand, glistening in the sunset. All those landscapes worked perfectly for their environment. So instead of looking at or even thinking about the grass on the other side, focus on finding the landscape that works perfectly for your life style.

April 12, 2013

Johnny Earle, founder of Johnny Cupcakes, told me today that "Autism is not a disability. It's a super power!" He has a fan and a customer for life in me!

April 15, 2013

Use your "good" dishes and towels today. Enjoy life now! Drinking Tang from champagne flutes with my little man.

April 18, 2013

I am trying to wait out an excited kindergartener who is sleeping lightly with one eye open hoping to catch a glimpse of the elusive Tooth Fairy. REM sleep, please come soon. Mama is so tired…

April 23, 2013

My little man told me that I am his favorite friend in the whole wide world! BAM! I'm about to live off that high for a while! You can't tell me nothing right now!

April 27, 2013

Ricky II should write a book: 1,000,001 Ways to Make Noise…

May 10, 2013

Volunteering in Ricky II's kindergarten class. The class gets loud, and the art teacher says, "Raise your right hand if you are sitting quietly. Raise your left hand if you are talking even though you are not supposed to." Student asks, "Which one is my left hand?" LOL!

May 11, 2013

I can't win for losing. Thank God I have a Super Kid! Got a notice from the post office that my travel wallet that I left in a hotel room in New Orleans a month ago had just been delivered. Jet outside to check the mail, lock myself out, again! This time no cell phone, and Ricky II is outside on the swing. I knock on our neighbor's door, and we end up hoisting Ricky II over our neighbor's deck on to ours. Ricky II saves the day! Now I have to unteach him to scale tall decks in a single bound from house to house…

May 12, 2013

Happy Mother's Day! If you are so fortunate to have had the wisdom of a mother to guide you through your life's journey, or the unconditional love of a mother to stand next to you in the hardest of times, consider yourself blessed beyond measure. I think I mourn not having the love and guidance of a mother more as a mother than I did as a child.

May 21, 2013

God is a door opener and a way maker! My village is top notch! Happy, Happy Tuesday!

May 23, 2013

I know in my heart that I am stronger than I feel today. Can the world stop spinning and let me get off and catch my breath? Just for a day...

May 28, 2013

Hearing my baby read is like listening to heaven's music. You go, Mama's Baby!

June 3, 2013

Not sure what this is, but I know a masterpiece when I see it! Pottery by Ricky II! #SuperKid

June 5, 2013

Mommy's little designer. Making a tye-dye shirt. After school fun!

June 5, 2013

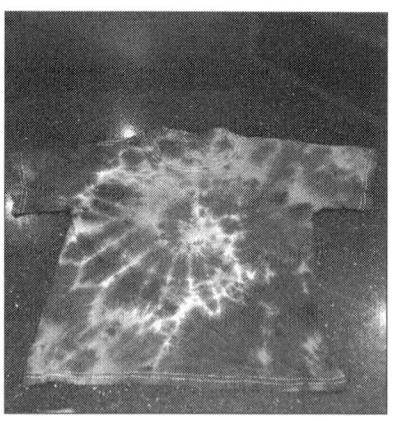

Designed by Ricky II! You go, Mama's Baby!

June 7, 2013

What are the chances that a friend I made in fourth grade would come back into my life 20+ years later and make a divine impact on the life of my school-aged child. God ALWAYS has a plan! My village is top notch! #Blessed #HoldMyMule

June 11, 2013

Yep, that telemarketer won't be calling here again. Ricky II answered the phone. She now knows his favorite color is purple, he had field day today, he is going to Florida this summer, he is growing mushrooms, he likes the big park, not the little one… She hung up on my baby in the middle of such a pleasant conversation. Telemarketers: 0; The Browns: 1 #Winning

June 17, 2013

I'm a great mom. Sometimes you just have to stop and pat yourself on the back. Watching my Super Kid at play. #ProudMommaMoment

June 18, 2013

School's out for my rising first grader! To celebrate, I asked him what he wanted to do after school. He said, "Go to the playground!" On the way to the playground, it started raining. "Oh no, Ricky II, what would you like to do now?" He answered, "Eat fried chicken!" *crickets*

June 19, 2013

Yep! Summer has officially begun. 9am and we're throwing water balloons off the deck.

June 19, 2013

Mommy's little reader!! Getting it in! Mommy Summer School is in session. #TeachersKid

June 27, 2013

On the way to summer camp, Ricky II and I were having a conversation about Stranger Danger because he is going on a field trip today for the first time, without a chaperone from our family. After the conversation, my baby thought for a second and then came back at me with, "Mommy, if I don't talk to strangers, how can I make new friends?" Um... O_O... My child is deep.

August 24, 2013

Summer is coming to an end, and after a successful year in kindergarten, I am preparing my mind for first grade. Although I have butterflies in my stomach, I know I have given him the tools to be successful. But before this school year begins, I want one day to just sit and reflect on the awesomeness of God and the blessing of being the mother of Ricky II. Lazy Saturday at the beach!

September 3, 2013

The first day of 1st grade! #BigBoySwag

September 3, 2013

Daddy and Ricky II! First Day of 1st Grade!!

Seven years old

September 19, 2013

Ricky II's birthday fruit kabobs for his classroom snack and story time celebration tomorrow! My baby's turning 7! Woot! Woot!

September 20, 2013

Happy Birthday to my favorite 7-year-old! This child is JOY personified! #LuckyMe

October 1, 2013

Coach Ricky II! LOL!

October 28, 2013

Meet Bobby the Gerbil! Ricky II's new pet!
#MayTheForceBeWithMe

December 10, 2013

My baby has just discovered "Ice, Ice Baby" and thinks he has found Hip Hop. Vanilla Ice has my child. If I hear a "Yo, VIP, let's kick it" one more time... O_O
#StopCollaborateAndListen

December 16, 2013

Ricky II just announced that he wants to celebrate Hanukkah this year. I wish he would have told me this before I finished Christmas shopping at Toys R Us today... O_O

December 25, 2013

Hundreds of dollars worth of gifts, and what is he most excited about? $25 velcro, light-up sneakers.

Ricky II: It looks like I have ambulances on my feet! Isn't that AWESOME!?

#IGiveUp #ShoppingSpreeAtTheDollarTreeNextYear

January 9, 2014

I'm the reason why teachers limit the amount of time they allow parents to volunteer in the classroom. My child just answered the question, "Can you name the two types of trees?"

Ricky II: Deciduous and Evergreen.

Me: *stands up, cheers, and old school happy dance*

Ricky II: O_O

#OhExcuseMeMyBad

#ThatsMyBaby

#OhOkaySureIllSitDownNow

January 11, 2014

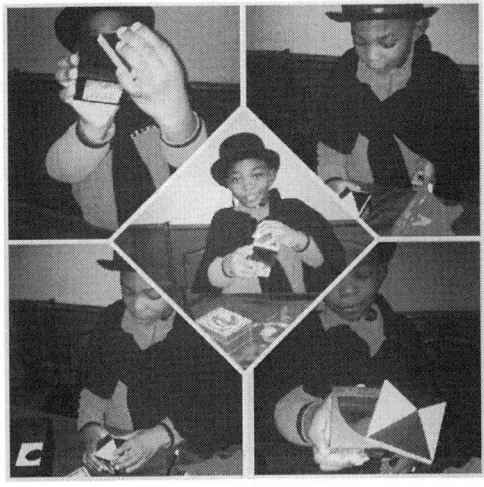

After four days of working as Ricky II the Great's trusted assistant, I am submitting my letter of resignation. I thought we were going the Harry Houdini route. Instead, he has chosen to go the route of The Incredible Burt Wonderstone and a host of YouTube street magicians. I draw the line at burning CDs in the family room in the name of "magic." #ImOut

January 16, 2014

Excuse me while I SHAMELESSLY BRAG on my Super Kid! Tonight's homework: Write two sentences about two important facts about Martin Luther King, Jr.

Me: Ricky II, give me one important fact about Martin Luther King, Jr.

Ricky II: He fought with his words. #BAM

January 26, 2014

Conversation with Ricky II:

Ricky II: Are all ladybugs girls?

Me: No, some are males.

Ricky II: That's wacky (his new word)! They should be called Manbugs or Daddybugs.

Me: If you like, we can call them coccinellidae.

Ricky II: Huh?

Me: Coccinellidae (clapping out the syllables) is another name for ladybugs.

Ricky II: I'm okay with "ladybug." *walks away*

#MyMamaIsATeacher #RandomInformation #WayExtra

February 7, 2014

Hoodwinked! I think I was just made an accessory to a master scheme to play hooky! From the school nurse's office to the skatepark. No signs of sickness. It's a BEAUTIFUL day. Can't say I blame him. #Whatevs #IAintMad

February 11, 2014

Just when I thought my day couldn't get any better, I get this email from Ricky II's teacher: "I have to share two of the sentences he created when we were working with the sight words this morning. The first word was 'am,' and he said, 'I am a super kid!' The second word was 'very,' and he said, 'I am very happy!'"

#MyPrideAndJoy

#MySuperKid

#TheSeedOfGreatnessHasTakenRoot

March 11, 2014

Okay! I can NOT make this stuff up! On the phone with Elyshia Hughes, my doorbell rings. Who is that at this time of night?

Me: Who is it?

Door: The Police.

I open the door. Two uniformed officers with flashlights are standing there.

Police: Ma'am, there was a 911 call from this address.

Me: No…

Police: Yes, Ma'am. Is everything okay?

Me: OH MY GOD! I have a seven-year-old. Ricky II! (Ricky II is in the stairwell looking guilty as sin.) Ricky II, did you call 911?

Ricky II: Gingerbread Boy.

Me: Officers, Gingerbread Boy is his imaginary friend. I am SO sorry.

Officer: Come here, little man. Are you okay?

Ricky II: Yes, but Gingerbread Boy got hurt.

Me: Officers, I am SO sorry.

Officer: It's okay, Ma'am. (To Ricky II) You should only call 911 if there is a real emergency.

Ricky II: (very matter-of-factly and pointing his finger at the officer) Gingerbread Boy broke his leg.

Officer: O_O

Me: Officers, I am SO sorry.

Elyshia: BAHAHAHAHAHA

Me: Elyshia, don't laugh! Officers, I am SO sorry.

Just another night at my house…

March 12, 2014

Ricky II just said to me, "Let's go to PetSmart and buy a stingray!" #MarinatingOnThatOne

March 24, 2014

My child just announced that he wanted to be a DJ. I can actually see that one. Time to get some turntables and earplugs. #PartyOvaHere

April 1, 2014

Ricky II is a master persuader. I just listened to him convince his best friend that Gingerbread Boy is real. So much so that his friend thinks he sees Gingerbread Boy too. At least now I know that Gingerbread Boy is small, but not tiny, about the size of Ricky II's shoe, brown, is 7 years old, and sitting on the table...

April 2, 2014

Today, I woke up extremely grateful that my son has a best friend (not Gingerbread Boy). A friend he chose and who chose him. They have their own little conversations, secrets, and a mutual adoration for each other. I have witnessed their relationship grow and develop over the last two years. It has been absolutely beautiful to watch. Whether you're 7 or 37 or 77, everyone deserves a best friend and running buddy. #LuckyHim #LuckyMe #LightItUp #MySuperKid

April 4, 2014

One evening after a particularly trying day, the weight of the world showed on my face. I said aloud to myself, "I've got this." A set of little eyes watched me closely, and a set of little ears heard my every thought. We got out of the car, and my Super Kid turned to me and said with a huge smile, "Mommy, you can be anything you want to be, if you plan and work hard!" The mantra that I gave to him at three years old, he gave back to me on the day I needed it most. #Empathy #LightItUp #ILoveMySuperKid #LuckyMe #AutismAwareness

April 11, 2014

Volunteered during recess at Ricky II's school. Umm, yeah, the kid swinging super high on the swings while belting out "Let It Go" from *Frozen* would be MINE. LOL! #HeKeepsItInteresting #ILoveMySuperKid #LightItUp

April 13, 2014

When my Super Kid was a little guy, I ALWAYS had a purse full of purple earplugs. Sensory Processing issues made it uncomfortable for him to be around loud sudden noises and flashing lights in contained spaces. I remember holding and soothing him in bowling alleys or having to leave restaurants that made him uncomfortable. Now I NEVER say no to Chuck-E-Cheese's because each time my Super Kid walks confidently into that busy black hole of tokens, tickets, flashing lights, bells, dings, sirens, and screaming little people, all I see is resilience, progress, and pure awesomeness! Now, I'm the one who wears the purple earplugs. LOL! #ILoveMySuperKid #LightItUp #AutismAwareness

April 14, 2014

One day shortly after my little guy began to find his words, he proudly said to me while in the commissary, "Ricky II eat yogurt in the woods." I said, "Okay" and kept pushing the cart down the aisle. He put his hand on my arm and said it again. He was obviously trying to tell me something. I stopped the cart and asked, "Would you like some yogurt?" He said, "No." I replied, "I'm sorry, Sweat Pea. Mommy doesn't understand."

I started to push the cart again. He said the sentence over and over again and began to get extremely frustrated, his little face turned red, and he started to cry. My heart broke because he was trying to tell me something. I could tell there was something he expected me to do, and I just didn't understand. I made a choice right then. I could have carted him out of the commissary for the comfort of others. I could have disciplined him for not using an "inside voice" in the store. Instead, I chose to step into my child's world and work through that moment with him. I may not have understood what he was trying to tell me, but he wouldn't go through this moment alone. I got him out the cart and sat right there on the commissary floor with him and let him say his sentence over and over again and told him we would stay right there until I understood or he was ready to move on. People walked around us, some gave a warm smile, some stared, others huffed. I didn't care. That moment was about me and my child and building a trusting relationship.

I didn't understand his request that day, but I made sure my baby understood that whatever was on his mind he could always tell Mama, and if I didn't understand, we would stop the world and I would listen and we would try to process it together. I needed him to know his words have value, and just because I couldn't understand them immediately, it didn't mean that what he had to say wasn't important.

Weeks later, I broke the code. He wanted vanilla pudding cups. He had eaten some at a play date we had in a friend's backyard. You better believe we went to Costco and bought vanilla pudding cups in BULK! #ILoveMySuperKid #LightItUpBlue #AutismAwareness

April 15, 2014

I understand that unless your life has been directly touched by autism, it is difficult to understand exactly what autism is. The public hears the word, but oftentimes it isn't attached to everyday families just living life. It's attached to a story of misfortune or extreme accomplishment. Most families touched by autism are just living our lives somewhere on the spectrum, loving our Super Kids.

April 15, 2014

My Super Kid was nonverbal until he was 4 years old. But I always heard him because instead of listening to him with my ears, I learned to listen to him with my heart. The blessing in that is I am now able to hear everything he says and DOES loud and clear. I hear EVERYTHING, and rarely miss ANYTHING, and that has made me a better and more engaged parent. #WeAreConnected #LuckyMe #ListenWithYourHeart #PositiveParentEngagement #ILoveMySuperKid #LightItUp

April 16, 2014

I often hear from people "Are you sure he has autism?" or "He doesn't look like he has autism."

Autism is a spectrum disorder, meaning that there is a wide degree of variation in the way it affects people. Every child on the autism spectrum has unique abilities, symptoms, and challenges.

Autism is not a single disorder, but a spectrum of closely related disorders with a shared core of symptoms. Every individual on the autism spectrum has challenges to some degree with social skills, empathy, communication, and flexible behavior. But the level of the challenge and the combination of symptoms varies tremendously from person to person. In fact, two kids with the same diagnosis may look very different when it comes to their behaviors and abilities. I recognize that no two individuals on the autism spectrum share the same journey, therefore, if I ever need to refer to my child or any other child in reference to their diagnosis I say, "_____ is a child on the Autism Spectrum." Please feel free to use the same phrasing to be certain to not offend a parent of a child on the spectrum or dishonor the individual journey of each child on the spectrum. #ILoveMySuperKid #LightItUp #AutismIsASpectrum #AutismAwareness

April 16, 2014

So... I am listening to Ricky II try to flirt with this cutie at the park named Nora. Despite his best efforts, all he has been able to get from her is her name. He has offered her his scooter (that's major). He has had me videotape him doing tricks on his scooter in front of her. My baby is bringing his A-Game, and Nora is not impressed... yet. #NorasParentsTaughtHerWell #HardToGet #MakeHimWork #TestosteroneIsHighUpInHere

April 17, 2014

I absolutely LOVE that Ricky II can spend an entire day outside and is completely entertained by his environment. The world is his Disney Land! Happy Spring Break, Little Man! #ILoveMySuperKid #LightItUp

April 18, 2014

Ricky II just announced to me that June 14 is Happy Day! He is already in Party Planning mode. Happy Day Party at The

Browns'!! Saturday, June 14th, mark your calendar! Woot! Woot! #MakingHisOwnHolidaysNow #IFeelATraditionStarting

April 18, 2014

Ricky II found a crew at the skate park. He swears he was hanging with the Big Boys! #RollinWitMyScooter #CanYouGuessHisDadsFrat #ILoveMySuperKid

April 18, 2014

Years ago, while visiting a good friend whom we hadn't seen in some years, she said to me, "El, I don't know how you do it. It must be so hard on you. You are so strong." I HONESTLY had no idea what she was talking about. But I assumed she may have been referring to starting a business while being a mother. As she went on, I realized she was referring to being the mother of a child on the autism spectrum.

"WHOA WHOA WHOA! Being Ricky II's mommy isn't hard. I only have one child, and I only know one way to be a mommy, and that is to be Ricky II's mommy. God gave me everything I need to give Ricky II everything he needs. I am lucky I was trusted to be his mommy. This isn't my journey; it's His. I'm just His guide."

My dear friend meant no harm by her statements. She only saw what appeared to be me working a little harder with my baby than she had to with hers, and she was concerned for her friend.

Fast forward two years, and one of her babies was diagnosed with cancer. In conversation, I said to her, "God prepared you to be your baby's mother. He equipped you with everything you need to meet your baby's need and make your baby happy and comfortable. All you have to do is be your baby's mommy. Your baby will be looking to you to know how he is supposed to feel about each day."

As she sat by her baby's bed, I am almost positive that her heart was so full with love for her baby that her mother's instinct told her exactly what to do and meeting her baby's needs came automatically. It wasn't work; it was LOVE.

#RIP

#GodChoosesSpecialPeopleForSpecialChildren

#AMothersLove

#ILoveOurSuperKids

#LightItUp

April 22, 2014

For about a week now Ricky II has been proclaiming that "_____ is my girlfriend." I tried to ignore this other female in my son's life by not acknowledging his proclamations. This morning he said it again, so I went in, rapid fire.

Me: Why is _____ your girlfriend?
Ricky II: Because I love her.
Me: Why do you love her?
Ricky II: Because she is pretty.
Me: Why is she pretty?
Ricky II: Because she is nice. She has pretty hair and wears pretty dresses.
#WellOkayThen
#IGuessHeToldMe
#PlayOnPlaya
#ILoveMySuperKid
#LightItUp

May 2, 2014

Conversation at today's pick up from school

Me: Hey, Sweet Pea! I missed you!
Ricky II: Hey... You look different
Me: Different? What do I look like?
Ricky II: You look pretty.
Me: Umm... Thank you? O_O
#WhatDidILookLikeBefore
#HeKeepsIt100
#GottaLoveMySuperKid

May 14, 2014

Just got best compliment EVER!

Ricky II: Do you like Frozen? *played in HEAVY rotation in our house*
Me: Yes *little white lie; sick of it*
Ricky II: Me too. You know what I like better than Frozen... is you.
Me: Me! You like me better than Frozen?
Ricky II: Yes, very much.
*falls asleep in my lap *
#SickDayChronicles
#UpSince4am
#NurseMommy
#ILoveMyJob

May 21, 2014

Yesterday on the drive home from school, Super Kid said to me, "Thank you, Mommy, for my house." Now if that kind of gratitude isn't a motivator to Go Get IT! I don't know what is!
#MyWhy
#MyCheerleader
#YourMamaGotThis
#ILoveMySuperKid — feeling invincible.

June 14, 2014

1st Annual Happy Day!!! Helping my SuperKid go from an idea to reality...makes me Happy!!! Ricky II's Happy Day was a Huge Success!!! #ilovemysuperkid #HappyDay

June 18, 2014

While getting ready for school, I hear Ricky II singing in the bathroom.

Me: Ricky II, are you brushing your teeth like I asked?
Ricky II: Perhaps.
#UmmIsThatSurburbanKidBackTalk
#SomebodyBettaGetHim

June 28, 2014

Me: Ricky II, can you get me another Fruit Roll Up?
Ricky II: No.

Me: Huh?

Ricky II: No. You don't need any more. Fruit Roll Up is a sometimes food.

#WompWomp

#UpSideMyHead

#WhenTheStudentBecomesTheTeacher

July 8, 2014

Hustling to get to the bus stop on time, because as per Ricky II's new rule, I am no longer allowed to pick him up in gym clothes because it makes him "sad." I have to wear a "pretty dress, smile, and smell good."

#TrophyMom

#ThisChild

#HisPoorWife

July 17, 2014

I guess a pretty dress, a smile, and smelling good wasn't enough. Ricky II just walked in the living room holding four-inch heels and said, "Wear these tomorrows at the bus stop." Umm, say what now?

#TrophyMom

#DontMakeMeOver

#ICanBarelyWalkInAStraightLineInFlats

July 18, 2014

About a month ago, a lady in the park started an unnecessary conversation with Ricky II. We were about to leave and he was asking for his water play container from a child he had let use it. The mother sitting by the fountain thought Ricky was taking the boy's container and said something to him then reached over to take the container from Ricky II. Not appreciating her manner, I got up from my blanket and called out "Ma'am!!! Uh-uh!!" I looked her square in her eyes while holding up a single finger.

Today, Ricky II and I were reading a chapter book, and the mother Anatosaurus let out a loud tuba sound when the little girl got too close to the nests that housed the baby dinosaurs. My reading comprehension question to Ricky II: What do you think the mother dinosaur was saying to Annie?

Ricky II: Ma'am! Uh-uh! *while holding up a single finger*
dead
#NobodyBetterMessWithMyBaby
#TeamMamaBear
#ILoveMySuperKid

July 19, 2014

Just been informed that the child formerly known as Super Kid is now SuperDuperKid. Carry on.
#MyChild
#NoSelfEsteemIssuesHere

July 25, 2014

I am always so touched by the kindness of teenagers when it comes to my SuperDuperKid. Today, he insisted on carrying Princess Anna and Queen Elsa in his shirt, much like I used to carry him in my Ergo Baby. A group of teenagers skateboarding and doing scooter tricks at the park took time to show Ricky II and some other little ones how to do scooter tricks. When Ricky II's scooter handles were loose, two of the teenagers knelt down and tightened it. I went over to say thank you. As they were leaving, one of the boys turned to me and said, "Ma'am, I like your son's Elsa and Anna dolls. *Frozen* is my favorite movie." My baby just BEAMED!
#IBelieveInOurYoungPeople
#ToTheBeatOfHisOwnDrum
#ISeeTheWorldThroughHisEyesEveryday
#luckyme

July 25, 2014

Since SuperDuperKid has to go to summer school at 7:30 each weekday morning, we made an agreement that we can do what he likes and stay up late on the weekend. While watching TV, he's on the couch with heavy eyes, nodding off...

Me: Ricky II, you need to go to bed. You're tired.
Ricky II: Is it the weekends? (Yes, that's plural.)
Me: Yes, but you are falling asleep.
Ricky II: I'm sleepy, but I want to stay up too. I'm going to ride my scooter for an energy break.
Translated: Turn Down for What #BoyGoToBed

July 31, 2014

SuperDuperKid Strikes Again! We pass by the painters every-day. I would have NEVER thought to ask them to let me paint the building, but then again, I'm not Super Duper Kid! He has left his mark on the neighborhood. #ImAFan #ILoveMySuperKid

August 17, 2014

Ms. Sarah, the kind and patient bird house volunteer, earned her hours today. Ricky II's fascination with birds coupled with his "Why" phase made for an hour of non-stop dialogue. God always sends GOOD PEOPLE into our space.
#FriendsWhereverHeGoes
#ILoveMySuperKid
#TrappedInTheBirdHouse

August 17, 2014

Ricky II was vacationing in FL for the past two weeks. While he was gone, I switched his peanut butter and jelly out for

natural peanut butter and fruit spread. Made him a sandwich today. He took a bite, looked at it suspiciously, took another bite, smelled it, then put the sandwich down and said to me, "I like my peanut butter and jelly the regular way."
#FAIL
#CantWinThemAll

September 2, 2014

First day of second grade! He was sooo ready. Apparently I WAS NOT! The teacher met us at the door and did not let us in. I WAS NOT READY! We had to take his pictures outside of the classroom, and I tried my best to fight back the tears. That lucky lady gets to spend all day with MY baby. God Bless and Keep My Child. Now I know how my students' parents felt when I stood at the door. He's a big boy now. Time is just moving way too fast. #IMissMySuperKid

September 2, 2014

After school conversation:

Me: Ricky II, what was your favorite part of the day?
Ricky II: Dismissal. No, recess! #MyChild

September 2, 2014

The sweetest thing in the world: hearing my seven-year-old sing the lullaby I have been singing to him since before he was born.

Ricky II, Ricky II,
Your mommy loves you.
Ricky II, Ricky II,
Your mommy loves you.
I love you. I love you.
I love you. I do.
Ricky II, Ricky II,
Your mommy loves you.

Eight years old

September 20, 2014

Thanks for My Child!!! Happy 8th Birthday, Ricky II!!! I am still in awe by you and so grateful that God selected me to be Your Mommy... To the moon and back... #ILoveMySuperKid

September 27, 2014

My baby just got up to the plate, turned to me in the stands, and said, "Mom, I got this." Then he hit that ball on the first pitch. Outta here! BOOM! #Praises #ImTheVoiceHeHears #RaisingConfidentKids #HeGotThis #BecauseHeSaidSo

October 5, 2014

I learn from this child every day! He never gives up. He is tenacity personified. He gets it from his mama. His mama got hers back by watching him. #WeGotThis #ILoveMySuperKid

October 5, 2014

I am not an expert on much, but trust and believe, I am the expert on all things Ricky II
-Signed Mama Bear #40WeeksUnderMyHeart #ALifetimeInIt

October 14, 2014

This child finds JOY wherever he goes. Picked him up from school, zipped across town to meet a deadline, set him down in a lobby chair with my iPhone, where he waited patiently. After all that frantic rushing on my part, cool as a cucumber, Ricky stops to play in the fall leaves on the way to the car. Stop and enjoy the moment. I want to be like Ricky II when I grow up. #ILoveMySuperKid

October 18, 2014

Ricky II requested an all-day outing with his friend and classmate today… a girl. They play very well together, so I thought nothing of it. Our night comes to an end and we take her home. After a short visit at her house…

Me: Ricky II, it's time to go. Let's say good-bye. Give _____ a hug or a high five.
Ricky II: Or a kiss…
#UmmSirLetsGo   #ThisWasNotADate   #IGottaWatchHim #YouAintSlick

October 31, 2014

It's Halloween morning and Ricky II has already submitted his Thanksgiving menu: turkey and fruit punch. DONE! #ImAllOverThat #KeepItSimple

October 31, 2014

After reviewing Ricky II's Trick or Treat bag from this evening's BOOtique event, I have come to realize he is a Trick or Treating lightweight. When reaching in the candy bowl, he would bypass the good candy for duds. I will be making "good candy" flash cards: Twix, Snickers, Reese's Cups, Almond Joy, Kit Kat. YES. Peppermint discs, Tootsie Rolls, Smarties, plain M&M's, 3 Musketeers. NO. #ThisIsNotAGame #BringHomeTheChocolate

November 1, 2014

Parenting Gripe. It doesn't happen often, but I gotta say it. Ricky II was SUPER excited about Halloween this year, so we went ALL IN. For two weeks straight we had been pumpkin picking, fall festival-ing, hay riding, haunted housing, pumpkin bread baking, scary bounce house jumping, carnival riding, costume wearing, kettle corn eating, apple bobbing, pumpkin slingshotting, Halloween partying, and Trick or Treating, all ending after 10pm last night after he requested dinner for him and his friend at a Chinese food restaurant. I am dog tired and just wanted a little sleep on a Saturday morning. This child wakes me up before 8am saying, "I'm bored. What are we doing today?" YOU HAVE GOT TO BE KIDDING ME! #ComeGetHim

November 1, 2014

Shutting it down for the night.

Me: Ricky II, if you wake up before me, don't wake me up.
Ricky II: Same thing for you.
Me: Huh?
Ricky II: If you wake up before me, don't wake me up.
#Speechless

November 5, 2014

After school, a teary-eyed Ricky II insisted that he put up a Christmas tree in his room today, instead of waiting until Thanksgiving night. Fall wreath on the door, pumpkin centerpiece on the counter top, and a Christmas tree. He did it all by himself. He's proud, I'm pleased, but I realize my child is WAY EXTRA.
#WeAreThosePeople
#ChristmasTheFirstWeekOfNovember
#ImJustAlongForTheRide

November 11, 2014

Just had the BEST IEP Meeting EVER! The Principal Designee said, "Let's table this meeting and have a discussion. Mrs. Brown, you are the expert on Ricky II. Tell us about Ricky

II so we can go back and develop goals that will help Ricky II become his best." She gets it! BOOM! She was the variable that changed the tone of that meeting. I LOVE her!
#FCPS #MovedToTears
#HappyMamaBear
#HeartSoFull
#ILoveMySuperKid

November 13, 2014

On the way to school morning conversation…

Ricky II: I don't want to go through Kiss and Ride today.
Me: Okay, why?
Ricky II: I want you to take me inside the school so everyone can see how pretty you look today.
#HesSoSmoothWithIt

#SomeonesGettingACarAt16
#ILoveMySuperKid

November 15, 2014

My childhood was extremely different from SDK's, so I experience so many "firsts" being his mommy. Today was my first time jumping in a pile of leaves. I would have never thought to do that. #ThroughMyBabysEyes #LivingOutLoud #Joy

November 17, 2014

May he ALWAYS be my baby. Last week Ricky II told me he wanted a toilet with "blue water." Today while out shopping I purchased a $2 disc to put in his toilet tank. When he got home, he went straight to the bathroom. I hear the toilet flush, then "Oh, WOW! It's amazing! You did it! Thank you, Mommy! It's like an ocean in my toilet!"
#HeThinksIHaveSuperPower

#AndILoveIt
#TheLittleThings
#We'reGoodAsLongAsHeDoesntDrinkIt

November 18, 2014

Before bed I commended SDK on being so well behaved during my three-hour class tonight.

Me: Thank you, Ricky II. I really appreciate how quiet and well behaved you were during Mommy's class tonight.
Ricky II: You're welcome. Gingerbread Boy was quiet too.
Me: Oh, Gingerbread Boy was there? Was he reading a book too?
Ricky II: Noooooo. Gingerbread Boy can't read. He's a cookie, Mommy. Cookies can't read. #FollowThatLogic

November 29, 2014

Ricky II's friend just told him there was no Santa Claus. He looked at her like she had an extra eye growing slap in the middle of her forehead. I had to step in and change that subject real quick. I guess she forgot that he is the same little boy who is BFFs with an invisible cookie named Gingerbread Boy. O_O

December 10, 2014

Parents of children with IEPs: Always remember that an IEP meeting is a team effort and YOU are the team captain. Teachers and schools have your Super Kid for a season. You have your Super Kid for a lifetime. You are the expert on your child in that room. Go to your child's IEP meeting prepared to participate in the discussion as opposed to listening to goals that someone else has developed for your child. Empower yourself by researching IEP goals and identifying some that suit your child. Make your own list of goals. Then at the meeting, collaborate with the team to tailor the goals to reflect the specific needs of and desired outcomes for your Super Kid. #YouGotThis #BeEmpowered #TeamMamaBear

December 17, 2014

Sometimes my heart still hurts a little bit when I drop him off at school. I miss SDK already.
#CoverMyChild
#ILoveMySuperKid
#MyBaby

December 21, 2014

I thought Mama Bear was a universal language. Luckily not only am I fluent in it, I can translate it in any language or dialect. I can even sign it or pantomime it if you can't hear me.
#ImSeriousAboutMyBaby
#LikeADogWithABone

December 23, 2014

SDK, the Super Sleuth

Ricky II: So… Santa is bringing my presents at Christmas.
Me: Yes.

Ricky II: And the elves left those presents under my tree...
(Pointing at the tree)
Me: Yes.
Ricky II: Soo... Did the elves use the wrapping paper in the closet? (Pointing at the hall closet)
Me: Umm... Yes?
#TheSetUp
#TheJigIsAlmostUp

January 4, 2015

Scripting! When Ricky II was learning to talk, his entire word bank and conversational phrases could be found in a box set of *Franklin and Friends* DVDs. Best speech therapy EVER! We <3 Franklin!
#CountByTwos
#AndTieHisShoes
#Coolio
#NickJr
#ILoveMySuperKid

January 4, 2015

I walked into the living room after getting dressed and Ricky II said, "You look like a super model!" We were heading out to dinner. Now we're heading out to dinner and Toys R Us! BOOM!
#ILoveMySuperKid
#HeGotMeWhipped
#StillBlushing

January 4, 2015

When I was a child, a snack for me was a Little Debbie Star Crunch, Zingers, Cheetos, or Poptarts. Happiness is watching your son eat freshly roasted kale chips while playing before bed, as the beets he requested for his after-school snack tomorrow are roasting in the oven. My change has become his lifestyle!
#RoleModel
#IAmMySonsMother
#BuildingHealthyHabits
#ILoveMySuperKid

January 8, 2015

Ricky II just called his friend on the phone.

Ricky II: Hey!
BF: Hey, Ricky II!
Ricky II: Where are you?
BF: I'm home.
Ricky II: You're home? Watcha doing?
BF: Nothing. Here with my mom. Watcha doing?
Ricky II: Here. Waiting on you.
BF: Ricky II, would you like me to come over to your house?
Ricky II: Yes!
BF: Okay. Let me ask my mom.
#SocialSkills
#Autism
#ParentsKeepPressing
#GodAnswersPrayers
#ILoveMySuperKid
#HeartSoFull

January 10, 2015

First conversation of the morning:

Me: Ricky II, you know what I'm going to do?
Ricky II: What?
Me: I'm going to write a book about you.
Ricky II: Thank you.
#YoureWelcome
#ConsiderItDone
#Boom
#ILoveMySuperKid
#MyChild
#MyPassion
#MyPurpose

January 12, 2015

Morning conversation:

Ricky II: Mom.
Me: Yes, Ricky II?
Ricky II: I want a flying, fiery dragon as a pet.
Me: No. You can't have a flying, fiery dragon as a pet.
Ricky II: Why?
Me: Because I don't know where to buy one.
Ricky II: Oh.
#MyChild #IfICouldIWould #ILoveMySuperKid

January 24, 2015

I've been gone for over a week. I asked Ricky II what he would like today. He said watch The Jungle Book and eat popcorn. After we had been sitting for a while:

Me: This was a good idea. I like hanging out with you, Ricky II.

Ricky II: I know, that's what you do when you like someone. You eat popcorn and watch TV with them. I missed you a whole lot.

Me: *swoons* <3

January 28, 2015

After reading our bedtime story, *You Can Do It* by Tony Dungy, a story about dreaming big and finding your "it":

Ricky II: What do you want to be when you grow up?
Me: Who me?
Ricky II: Yes.
Me: Well, hmm I want to help adults be good parents and teachers.
#AndThereYouHaveIt
#AskingTheHardQuestions
#ILoveMySuperKid

Bedtime Conversation Part 2:

Ricky II: Ask me what I want to be when I grow up.
Me: Okay, what do you want to be when you grow up?
Ricky II: I still wanna be a doctor, but I really want to be me.
Me: LOL! Okay, I like that! I think that's a wonderful idea because you're perfect!
Ricky II: I know. *straight face* *dead serious*
#BOOM #HeBettaSayThat #OwnIt #ILoveMySuperKid

February 6, 2015

There's nothing I won't do for my son. #SwallowingMyPride #MommyWillFixIt

February 7, 2015

Man, I tell you I want to be like Ricky II when I grow up! He likes to stay in the Embassy Suites when he travels because of the breakfast in the morning (all you can eat bacon) and the indoor pool. Well, we check in and there is NO POOL. I'm annoyed, but Ricky II says, "I still like this hotel. I have a nice view from my window," then proceeds to play with the water in the bathroom. Oh, to be like that child, swim trunks on, enjoying his life.

#LuckyMe
#IGetToBeHisMommy
#ILoveMySuperKid

February 17, 2015

Still in awe as I watch him sleep. All that awesomeness came from inside of me. *smitten*

February 20, 2015

Today I am reflecting on the goodness, purity, and perfection that is SDK. Wednesday I was working on a presentation, and while compiling "Before" pictures to illustrate my 100 pound weight loss, Ricky II looked on my screen and saw this pic.

Ricky II: Who are those ladies?
Me: Which ones? (assuming there was a possibility he didn't recognize me)
Ricky II: Those two. (pointing to the ladies on either side of me)
Me: That's Melissa and Chasette. They were with us in California. This is when they came to visit us at our old house in Fairfax.
Ricky II: Oh.
Me: Who is that? (pointing to me)
Ricky II: That's Mommy! (laughing)

Me: Do you notice anything different about Mommy now and Mommy in the picture?
Ricky II: Yes, you are wearing glasses, and you're not wearing glasses now.

All he sees is love. I don't know what I did to deserve the blessing of being SDK's mother, but I thank God EVERY DAY for choosing me. #LuckyMe

February 21, 2015

Ricky II has been fascinated with the human brain ever since our trip to the Franklin Institute. While watching a YouTube video on the human brain and its components and functions, Ricky II calls out to me:

Mom!
Me: Yes, Ricky II?
Ricky II: When I grow up I want to be a Brain Surgery Man.
Me: It's called a Brain Surgeon.
Ricky II: Oh, when I grow up I want to be a Brain Surgeon.
Me: Okay, that sounds like a plan. I will do whatever I can to help you.
Ricky II: Thank you! First we are going to need to do lots of practice!
Me: Umm… O_O #SoByPracticeWhatExactlyDoYouMean

February 22, 2015

Teenagers get a bad rap sometimes, but I can honestly say I encounter courteous, considerate, patient, and thoughtful teenagers whenever I am out with Ricky II. Yesterday he and a friend were playing in the snow, and a group of "rowdy" teenagers came with their horseplay. Ricky II watched them, completely fascinated by the "big kids." After a while, he walked up to them and said, "You wanna have a snowball fight?" And they said, "Of course!" They stopped what they were doing and gave Ricky II and his friend their attention. It was the most beautiful snowball fight, and Ricky II's chest swelled with pride.

#ThankYou
#GreatKids
#KudosToTheirParents
#RaisingAmazing

March 6, 2015

It is absolutely no fun watching slapstick comedy with Ricky II.

Ricky II: It's not funny when someone falls.
Me: You're right…
Ricky II: It's not nice to take a little girl's bike.
Me: You're right…
Ricky II: You shouldn't laugh when someone crashes into a truck. That's dangerous.
Me: You're right…

#NoMoreModernFamilyWithYou
#BuzzKill
#EtiquettePolice
#WhenMannersGoWrong

March 6, 2015

Today I thank God for Parents' Place in Pacific Grove, CA. A new mommy of a 4-week-old, I was utterly exhausted, and I felt nothing like myself. I was a stay-at-home mom, and SDK and I were stuck in the house every day. Other than love him, feed him, and keep him clean, I really didn't know what to do with him. I was a little afraid of how I was feeling, so I made an appointment with my primary care physician. After I explained to him how my body and mind were feeling, he responded by asking, "Have you always been chubby?" Then he proceeded to lecture me on the benefits of a healthy weight. I was BLOWN. What little energy I had, he just snatched it out of me. I got off his table and picked up SDK's carrier with tears in my eyes. I knew I couldn't go home.

In Lamaze class and at my maternity photo session, I was told about the place called Parents' Place. Of course I didn't think I would need it at the time because I was going to be Super Mom. But I filed the information away in my head anyway. I am so glad I did. I left the doctor's office and drove teary-eyed to the safe haven of Parents' Place. They took me and Baby SDK in that day. Their policy was they never turned away a mom with a baby 3 months old or under, such a critical age. For the next 3 years, SDK and I went to Parents' Place every week, several times a week for our mommy and me activities, parent education, and playgroups. I am still friends with my circle of mommy friends and teachers from Parents' Place—my village.

Motherhood can be isolating. Link into a network if you feel yourself getting overwhelmed at any stage of parenting. We are all in this world together. We got this.
#ItTakesAVillage #ToRaiseAMommy

March 26, 2015

After nine days in Africa I got my baby BACK!!! And he's wearing glasses! His teacher told me his prediction for my return was, "My mom is going to hug me and never let go." He knows me so well! LOL! #ILoveMySuperDuperKid #SDK #Reunited #AllIsRightInTheWorld #MySonShine

April 5, 2015

My church stays packed, and on Easter Sunday, keeps a line wrapped around the church for all services. So when I received an invitation to attend a friend's church for Easter Sunday, I eagerly accepted. This morning SDK told me he wanted to attend children's church. I said okay but understood at a new church that would mean I would be camped out in the back of the room watching over my baby. While getting out of the car, he said to me, "I want to go in all by myself." (He knows his mama.) I asked him if he was sure. He said yes, and my nervousness started. Over the next few minutes while waiting in line for children's church, I'm certain I asked SDK at least 5 more times if he was sure and offered to have him sit with me in the sanctuary. He excitedly assured me he wanted to go in by himself. During this time, I was battling with the caution that comes with being a parent of a child on the autism spectrum, while ensuring that I maintained an outward demeanor that communicated to SDK that I believed he had the ability to navigate this new social environment without me. We got to the visitors' desk and were greeted by someone in the Children's Ministry. She instructed me to fill out the visitors' registration form. As I filled out the form, there was a field for "Any Special Needs." I wrote in "ASD." I still didn't want to let my child go, but by that time he was GONE, playing with the kids inside. I turned to the Children's Ministry volunteer who had greeted us.

Me: My son has Autism Spectrum Disorder.

Her: Okay. Is he verbal or nonverbal?

Me: Verbal.

Her: Okay. Some of our children keep a special toy with them for comfort. Does he have a special toy?

Me: (pleasantly shocked by her demeanor, knowledge, and comfort about the subject) Yes! He has Wylie the Wolf with him. What's your name?

Her: Ms. Sharon.

Me: Ms. Sharon! Give it to me! *High Five* You are ON IT! Thank you! *choking back tears*

Ms. Sharon: *hugs* Enjoy service. We'll take good care of him.

I'm still not done crying.

#AngelsInOurCamp

#Progress #AutismAcceptance

#TrainYourVolunteers
#HeartSoFull
#ILoveMySuperKid
#AndILoveMsSharonToo
#HappyEaster
— feeling safe

April 8, 2015

This morning while getting ready for school, SDK looked at the pattern on his shirt and said, "This is tie dye, but it actually looks like Brain Synapses." BOOM! Make those STEM connections, Baby!
#ILoveMySuperKid
#ScienceAllAroundUs

April 24, 2015

TEAMWORK!!! The theme of this morning's IEP Meeting! BOOM!
#Winning
#HisVillageIsTopNotch
#TeamSDK
#CaptainMamaBear

April 29, 2015

It is no secret that I am completely in love with Ricky II. The thing I am proudest of in this world is God seeing me worthy to be his mommy. Ricky II is a faith and prayer baby. Pregnancies were extremely difficult for me. Ricky II was one of a pair of twins, and we lost two of his younger siblings.

While on bedrest with Ricky II, I stayed in faithful conversation with God.

"Father, if you see fit to deliver this child safely to my arms, I promise on everything in me that I will protect and nurture his soul. I know he is Yours, but if You just let me borrow him on earth, I promise I will protect and love him with everything in me. I will be the best mommy ever."

God answered that continuous prayer.

One morning when Ricky II was 19 months old and I was on my 3rd pregnancy, I placed him in his high chair to feed him breakfast. The house was very quiet. Big Ricky had deployed to Iraq a couple of months before, and Ricky II was completely nonverbal. But he spoke to me loud and clear with his eyes that morning as I fed him. I saw him say, "I love you, Mommy." I put down the spoon and replied, "I love you so much, Ricky II, and am so happy that you are here and so proud to be your mommy." My next statement caught me off guard. I continued, "You are all that I need. I am grateful and satisfied. Thank you, Father God, for my baby."—an odd statement for a woman with child.

After breakfast I took Ricky II to hourly care. I had a routine OB-GYN appointment. On the doctor's table, I was told there was no heartbeat. I had what would be my final miscarriage. I sobbed and drove directly to the CDC, grabbed my child, and darn near squeezed the breath out of him. Since that moment, Ricky II and I have been rolling HARD! I keep pompoms in my hands and a song in my heart when it comes to that child.

Yesterday, he got his report card, and I did the Happy Report Card Dance and Rap. Sometimes, I think I embarrass him, but every time I celebrate Ricky II, it is also a conversation of gratitude between God and me.

Well, last night at bedtime, Ricky II said, "Mommy, you can come sleep with me if you want to."
I laughed. "Oh, really?"
"Yes."

I heard something in his little voice (I am extremely fluent in Ricky II), so I shut the house down and got in bed with my baby. My eight year old cuddled up under me like a baby. I loved it and held him closer. His shoulders started to shake, and I felt something wet on my arm.

"Ricky II, are you crying?"
"Yes."
"What's wrong?"
"Nothing."
"Sweet Pea, you can tell mommy anything. Are you sad? Are you hurt?"
"No, I'm happy."
"You're crying because you're happy? Are you sure those are happy tears?"
"Yes."
"Well, what are you so happy about?"
"I can't tell you."
"You can tell me anything and I will listen. What is it about?"
"You."
"Me? What about me?"

"You are the most super mom in the whole world."

Gasps "SWEET PEA! Thank you! I love you so much, Ricky II."

"Will you hold my hand and squeeze it?"

"Of course, I will. Goodnight, Sweet Pea. Mommy loves you, and I thank God every day that you are here."

"Goodnight, Mommy."

Before I got into bed with Ricky II last night, I knelt down and said a prayer for our little family. God is still in the prayer-answering business.

#PraiseHim #IAmSoThankful #ILoveMySuperKid

May 2, 2015

Yeah... It's pretty official now!!! It's a bird... It's a plane... NOOOO... It's SuperDuperKid!!!!

#BOOM #POW #BAM #MyBaby #ILoveMySuperDuperKid

May 4, 2015

I'm the proud mom of a kid who goes to school wearing a Super Kid cape. Do you, SDK! - signed Your Biggest Fan

May 5, 2015

Sunday morning on the way to church, I had a conversation with SDK that I have been carrying in my heart. "Jesus Is Real" was playing in the car.

Ricky II: Is Jesus real?

Me: Yes.

Ricky II: Jesus is not imaginary?

Me: No, Jesus is real.

Ricky II: But you can't see Him?

Me: No, you can't see Him. But He's always there. Sometimes, you are away from Mommy and you know I'm still there because you can hear my voice in your head saying, "Ricky II, you are a Super Kid. Ricky II, I love you. Ricky II, be nice to your friends. Ricky II, don't eat all those cookies or you will get a tummy ache." Sometimes when you are at school or with Dad, you can still feel my hugs, kisses, and tickles. Right?

Ricky II: Yes!

Me: I can hear and feel Jesus even though I can't see Him. That's how I know He's real.

Ricky II: Oh, okay.

Seed planted. The soil is primed.

#ILoveMySuperKid #TheSoulGodEntrustedToMe

Jesus is real!

I can feel Him in my hands,

I can feel Him in my feet,

I can feel the Lord, God, Jesus all over me
I can feel Him in my heart,
I can feel Him in my soul,
I can even feel Him from the crown of my head to my toes.

May 7, 2015

The squeaky wheel gets the oil, and a closed mouth doesn't get fed. Parents, we have to speak up for our babies!
#WeAreTheirVoice

May 7, 2015

"Your Job is to Keep the Light On"

When SDK was 15 months old, our little family went to live in Junction City, KS, for two and a half months. Though our time there was short, my experience while in Kansas tremendously shaped the way I parent SDK. Shortly after we arrived in Kansas, I scheduled a routine baby appointment for SDK at the local military hospital. The visit and the experience with that doctor is one of my three lowest parenting moments. I walked out of that hospital feeling as though I had placed my child in a situation where his dignity was compromised. I put him in his car seat, got in the truck, called a good friend in Monterey, and cried like a baby. At the end of that conversation, after I wiped away the tears, my alter ego was born: Mama Bear! Never again. Not on my watch. On everything I love!

After that doctor's visit, I became hypersensitive about all things SDK. I didn't really take time to enjoy being a parent anymore. I had lasered in on my son's development, and I was in serious problem-solving mode. I was there, but I was a million miles away. One day, we took a day trip to Lawrence, KS. It was the dead of winter, and I was in search of an indoor play facility for SDK. After a couple of stops, we landed at a mall with a soft play area. We put SDK down. His father shadowed him. SDK wasn't a walker yet. We had learned to compensate for any areas where he might have difficulty. We did this without thinking. He was our first child, and we were (and are) completely enamored with all things SDK. But on this day, I looked at SDK with my teacher eyes for the first time. And I became very afraid. I watched his movements. I watched his lack of eye contact. I watched his lack of communication. And I watched all the other children around him. My son was there, but he was alone.

I am a deep thinker, and when I get lost in my thoughts, I can only imagine what my face must look like. On this day, I'm sure it was a combination of worry, fear, frustration, and determination as I stood tracking my son's every move. Whatever my look was, it was enough to prompt a grandmother in the play area to walk up to me and start a conversation[1] that would forever change the way I parent SDK.

She asked me if SDK was my only child. I answered yes. She said, "Oh, he's such a happy little guy." Then she said, "You love him so much. I can see from the way you look at him."

---

1 The conversation in the original social media post is described differently. Changes here reflect more accurately what was said that day.

I said, "I do. I really do, and I just want what's best for him all the time."

I told her I was a little concerned that he wasn't making any attempts to walk. She told me something in that conversation that to this day I carry with me, and I share with other parents as well. She said:

"Things go on with kids all the time. I'm not a doctor, I'm just a mom, but I've raised five kids, and I have grandkids as well. When you look at a child and there's a light in their eyes, know as a mom that everything's going to be okay. Your job as mom is to make sure that light always stays on." She said, "Your baby has a light. Now you make sure you keep it on."

Then she hugged me and walked away. I'll never know her name. We came from two different worlds, two different generations of moms. But she recognized in me what parents who have walked this walk can recognize from across a crowded room in an instant.

She was my angel. Wherever she is in this world, I invite her into my celebration of today's victory. I kept the light ON! I didn't listen to what any doctor, study, or well-intentioned family member or friend said. I became the expert on my child because I was tasked with keeping the light ON!

This morning I saw a light so bright in SDK's eyes, I am still emotional at the thought of it. I read his proposed IEP goals for next year a couple of weeks ago, and of course I wasn't satisfied. So I walked into the IEP meeting with my own goals and my own mission: to keep the light on! The goal that troubled me the most was a writing goal. The goal essentially referenced difficulty in writing complete thoughts. As Mama Bear, I never look at SDK with eyes of comparison. So I never concern myself with the expectations of a chronological or developmental age when it comes to my child. Every day, I aim to meet him where he is and provide for him the absolute best environment and conditions for success. I celebrate PROGRESS! With that said, I asked the IEP team, "Is the goal to have Ricky II write on paper with a pencil, or is the goal for him to communicate his thoughts so you can assess his knowledge and understanding?"

Some children on the spectrum learn and execute skills in isolation. Too many executive functions going on at one time, and they may shut down (or in some cases melt down). I proposed that SDK have another medium in school to produce his thoughts once generated. I told them I had researched the use of a tablet in school in our district and purchased an iPad for in-school use to assist him. I reasoned that if SDK could type or speak the answers to his assignments, he would stay focused because he wasn't exhausting all of his executive functions, and his teacher would have a better opportunity to accurately assess and evaluate knowledge and skills. SDK has only been speaking for four years. Therefore, his rate of progress is OUTSTANDING! It is up to us—parents, school, and teachers—to create the least restrictive environment for SDK to have every opportunity for success. On my watch, my child WILL succeed, and the light will stay ON!

His teachers jumped onboard! One of his teachers further

researched and found the app Co:Writer! Praise Father God! I purchased and downloaded it to his iPad and watched the light in my baby's eyes illuminate our entire home. He will be using the app for both school and homework! Look at God!

Signed,
Mama Bear, tasked with Keeping the Light ON!

May 8, 2015

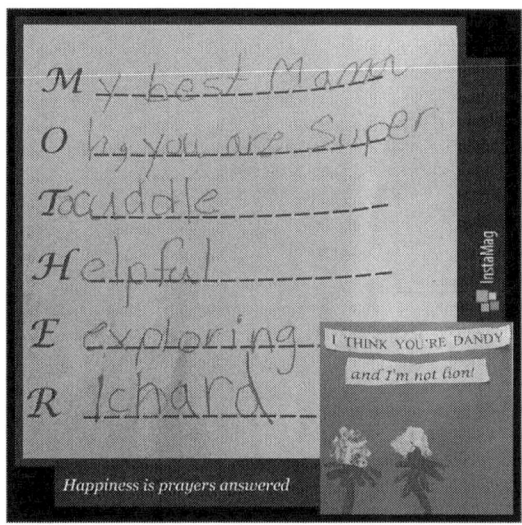

My two favorite holidays are Mother's Day and Thanksgiving, both for the same reason: I am so thankful that God chose me to be SDK's mother. SDK walks around as evidence of my most desperate prayer answered.
#SoThankful
#MothersDayWeekend2015

May 9, 2015

I decided to make Mother's Day Weekend all about the reason I am a mother... SDK! So last weekend, I asked him what he wanted to do. Without hesitation, he said, "Ride a pony!" Well, pony riding and a day at the horse farm it is! Happy Making Me a Mother Day, SDK!

#MommyAndMeLoveFest
#MothersDayWeekend2015
#ILoveMySuperDuperKid
#Motherhood

May 13, 2015

So, SDK no longer eats peanut butter and jelly in his lunch (I knew it was too good and easy to last). Last night at the grocery store, I suggested several alternatives. We agreed on turkey. After school conversation:

Me: How was lunch?

Ricky II: Okay.

Me: Just okay?

Ricky II: Yeah. Just okay.

Me: Did you eat your turkey sandwich?

Ricky II: No. I don't like that turkey. I like roasted turkey like you make in the oven, not flat turkey.

Me: Oh, I only make turkey like that for Thanksgiving.

Ricky II: And for my lunch.

May 13, 2015

You want turkey, you cook turkey! Earning his keep. Today we discovered onions burn your eyes when you cut them. Now to find out why! #CookingIsScience #MommysLittleChef

May 15, 2015

Early morning conversation:

Me: Ricky II, are you happy with your life?
Ricky II: Yes. Really happy.
#AskTheImportantQuestions #Childhood

May 16, 2015

SDK and Mommy take Manhattan!
#FieldTrip
#MommyAndMe
#TheWorldIsOurClassroom
#NYC

May 17, 2015

The Empire State Building

SDK and I just had the most beautiful day in New York City. I decided to go on impulse because he really wanted to see the Empire State Building (Madagascar 3 LOL!). I didn't check the weather report before buying our tickets. Thursday night there was a 60% probability of rain, and by Friday night the probability was 90%. I still decided to go. We dressed appropriately, and I prepped SDK with a talk. "Even if it rains, we are going to go and have fun because we are prepared for the weather." It was raining when we reached NYC, and it stopped right before we got off the bus. God held those storm clouds all day. And as soon as we left NYC, it started to pour, but we were sheltered on our bus.

This trip was so indicative of my life. I prepare for the storms and fully intend on showing up for life with praise in my heart and enjoying every minute of my life regardless of the probability of storms. I don't hide out and wait or hope for the storm to pass. Through my experiences I have learned more times than not that my God will hold back those storm clouds and allow me to enjoy the uninterrupted beauty of life even though every indicator may point to stormy days.

Stormy days ahead? Put on a rain coat and boots and be prepared to happily stomp in puddles. But know that God may decide to give you sunshine despite the visible storm clouds, so layer up!

May 27, 2015

In late March 2013, I took a then kindergartener SDK to his first day of Spring Break camp. By the end of the second day, he told me he didn't want to go back. When I asked him why, he said he had no friends and no one would play with him. In that moment, as a mommy, I had a decision to make: 1) keep my baby home and close to me, 2) send him to camp anyway (it WAS pricey and already paid for), or 3) pack a lunch, accompany him to camp, and investigate. I chose 3.

I didn't walk in to the camp as just SDK's mom. My master's degree is in Early Childhood Education, and I am well trained and experienced in conducting objective observations. I simply wanted to see and understand what SDK was experiencing during his day so I could better help him develop strategies to cope with his new environment. What I observed was young camp counselors working with young children with diverse personalities. I also observed some kids, to include my own, getting a little lost in the shuffle.

After a couple of hours of observation came art time. I watched young SDK paint a paper mache doll. He was pleased with his doll and his painting. However, it didn't meet the standard of another child in the group. That child proceeded to whisper to some of the other children. "Look at his doll. It's all messy." Some of the children ignored her. Others seemed uncomfortable. At this point, I got up from my chair and walked over to one of the little girls (who appeared to be in about 2nd grade) at his paint table and said, "I love your doll. It is very beautiful." I continued by pointing out all of the unique detailing she had carefully painted on her doll. She proudly smiled and said, "Thank you!"

I moved to the next child and gave specific recognition and praise for her artwork. The kids joined in offering their own compliments. Next I moved to SDK. I pointed out all of the unique details of his artwork. The child who was whispering earlier said, "But he did it wrong. His doll doesn't have any eyes." Before I could respond, the first little girl whose artwork I praised said, "It's art. There's no right or wrong. It's creative." (BOOM!) I answered, "I agree." SDK beamed with pride. The other children started complimenting each other's artwork, and just like that, the tone of the table was changed.

It didn't take much—just being aware. I had a brief conversation with the camp counselor and left satisfied, and with a child happily participating in camp and a kind-hearted camp counselor with a new sense of awareness.

After that camp experience, I wrote a song, *Friendship Numbers*, promoting inclusive play that we use in our KinderJam classes. I also called up my friend and said, "I'm going to develop a training for facilitating inclusive play in camps for camp counselors." No marketing plan—I just put it out in the universe.

Then life happened. My attentions went elsewhere, or so I thought, until an hour ago when it dawned on me that I am preparing for a training tomorrow for summer camp counselors on the subjects of Using Music, Chants, and Rhythm for Classroom Management *and*... wait for it! ... Facilitating Inclusive Play for Young Children. BOOM! Look At God! #WontHeDoIt #WalkingInMyPurpose #ILoveMySuperKid

June 19, 2015

Ricky wanted to be picked up early on the last day of school so he could hear his name over the classroom intercom, and his dad did it. "Ms. Cole, please send Ricky II to the office for early pick-up." BOOM!
#ItsTheLittleThings
#MakingMemories
#ChildhoodIsAhappyTime

June 19, 2015

SDK's Last Day of School!!! My Last Kiss to a 2nd Grader!!!
#MommyBigBoy #ILoveMySuperDuperKid

June 25, 2015

SDK and Mommy got a Selfie Stick!!! It's ON now!!!!! BOOM!!!! ❤❤❤

July 9, 2015

SDK walks into the kitchen to show me the umpteenth Minecraft YouTube video of the day.

Ricky II : Hey, Mom! Check this out!

Me: Oh, wow.

Ricky II: Don't say "Oh, wow."

Me: Why not?

Ricky II: Because when you say "Oh, wow" that means you're not listening to me.

#ColdBusted

July 10, 2015

Umm, so yeah, okay. All week long SDK has been telling me he wants me to take him to the park on Friday night to catch fireflies. I told him, "Okay. It's a date!" Then about an hour before we were set to leave, he asked me if he could bring a friend. "Okay, I'll check to see if she is home." We got to the park just after dark, hunting fireflies. As the night progressed, I began to realize I was the third wheel. SDK would say something, and I'd ask him what he said, and he would politely tell me he was talking to his friend. Then he asked me to take them to get something to eat. I looked up and saw hand-holding. Lastly, he ended the night with the SWEETEST little conversation at her door. At that moment, I realized one of us had a date on a Friday night, but it wasn't me. #MyChild #HesGotItBad

July 14, 2015

In Target picking up items on SDK's grocery list—pears, strawberries, and peanut butter balance bars. I grabbed a box of bars…

Ricky II: Get three boxes.

Me: No. We don't need three boxes.

Ricky II: We need a lot so we don't run out fast.

Me: No, three is too many.

Ricky II: Okay, let's get two.

Me: *blank stare*

Ricky II: Pleeeaaase. *looking all cute and stuff*

Me: Boy, you need a job. *as I toss two boxes in the basket*

Ricky II: My job is to play.

#MyChild

July 15, 2015

Learning on the GO!!!

Sometimes SDK shocks me with the things he remembers. Yesterday, he said, "Remember when we used to look for the green car, tall buildings, and the cow?" Huh? It took a couple of repeats for me to realize what he was talking about. Oh! Scavenger hunts! When he was in kindergarten, we had a 45-minute drive to spring break camp every day. At that time, SDK was still developing his language skills, so it was a challenge to maintain a conversation in the car with limited eye contact and nonverbal prompts. However, if I gave him a scavenger hunt, we could talk about the concrete items on his scavenger list. I looked through my things and found his old scavenger hunt list! I had it ready for our outing today. How amazing to watch the progress that has occurred since kindergarten. He could read the list instead of using the picture clues, he found the items quickly, and our conversation was so rich as he experienced the excitement of finding each item! To God be the Glory! #LearningOnTheGo #Progress #ILoveMySuperKid

July 20, 2015

Conversation as we are walking to the bus stop to meet the bus for summer school this morning...

Me: Come on, My SuperKid! Come on, My Amazing Kid! Come on, My Funny Kid! Come on, My Wonderful Kid! Alrighty, SuperKid... Have a WONDERFUL day at school today. Make SUPER decisions. I'll be there to pick you up at 11 o'clock. I love you more than anything in this whole wide world. *kiss kiss*

R2: I love you, My Super Mommy. You have an awesome day! Bye!!! I love you!!!

Me:❤❤❤

#ICoverHimWithLoveEveryday

#TodayHeCoveredMe

#ItsGonnaBeAGreatDay

#ILoveMySuperKid

#HeCalledMeHisSuperMommy

#BOOM

#Winning

July 21, 2015

Watching a YouTube video of kids playing at an indoor play facility:

Ricky II: Mom, instead of going to the fountains today, can we go here? *pointing to the video*

Me: Son, that's in Mallorca, Spain.

Ricky II: Oh. So can we go?

Me: No, you have summer school tomorrow... O_O

July 21, 2015

A Perfect Date with the Perfect Date

Man! I just love everything about this kid. Every experience is an adventure through his eyes. He loved Peter Pan 360 and was on the edge of his seat and asking questions the entire time. His excitement was so palpable that during the curtain call, one of the Lost Boys gave SDK a fist bump, and Captain Hook reached out to SDK so he could shake his hook. The gleam of amazement in SDK's eyes brought a tear to mine. I still can't believe I played a part in creating someone so perfect!

July 30, 2015

After watching the Sandra Bland 52-minute dash cam video, I purposely did not say anything about that incident. It just hit too close to home, and I had difficulty processing that a lane change without a blinker and a conversation that didn't go the way a policeman expected it to led to her death.

That video shook me at my deepest core. Looking at me, one may easily come to the seemingly obvious conclusion that it disturbed me so much because I am Black and female and have many parallels to the late Ms. Bland. But that would not be an accurate assumption. We all have filters by which we see the world. These filters are developed by our life experiences and determine what issues we feel passionate about and the topics that we find important, the things that prompt us into action. I have been Black and female all of my life, but those are not the filters by which I see the world. I can understand a Black person's perspective because of my life experiences as a Black American. I can understand a female's perspective because I am female. But the filter by which I see the world is that of a mom of a son on the autism spectrum. My every thought and action is somehow filtered through my experience as a mom of a son on the autism spectrum. My experience as SDK's mom dictates how I see the world.

SDK is what many consider high functioning. Which means in many ways his life will look no different than that of a typically developed adult when he comes of age. He will go to college, get a trade, or start a business. He will make friends, fall in love, get married, and make me a grandma one day. He will buy a car, a home, and support and protect his family. All because his father and I work tirelessly to groom him for greatness, support him without end as he journeys to maximize his personal potential, and love and cover him with a love so fierce that he wakes up every morning with the unequivocal belief and understanding that he is a super individual destined for greatness.

My son will achieve the highest of heights, and he will still be a man on the autism spectrum. What this means to my family is our son may look on the outside like everyone else but may always be a little socially different and process information differently than expected of him by someone who doesn't have an intimate knowledge and understanding of SDK or autism. He may not say the most appropriate thing during social interactions with people. He may not be aware of another's personal space, boundaries, or escalating emotions. There may be a pause before he answers a question. He may not make eye contact with the person speaking to him or the person to whom he is speaking. He may make involuntary hand gestures that coincide with his emotions as he processes his feelings. He may laugh at seemingly inappropriate times. He may answer a question unfiltered and with blatant honesty. He may not understand the layers of an interaction with the police or comprehend the danger that could be there for him as a Black man if he does not carefully navigate a seemingly routine stop or conversation. A policeman, not knowing, caring, or understanding with whom they are interacting may read my son's responses as disrespectful or potentially "dangerous." As a mom of a son on the autism spectrum, I need policemen to simply perform their jobs as written. I teach my son through concrete concepts, and if a policeman goes off script, my man child may not know what to do in that moment to de- escalate a potentially fatal interaction.

The Sandra Bland dash cam video shook me to my core because it was then that I realized that one day we are going to have to have "The Talk" with our son. The Talk where we give him a script and together help him commit it to memory. We are going to have to teach our son, if stopped by police, to raise his hands slowly yet immediately and say in the most gentle manner possible, "Officer, my name is Richard Franklin Brown II. I have autism and may not be able to communicate with you in the manner expected. Can you please use my phone to call my wife, mom, or dad so they can assist?"

And that breaks my heart.

August 7, 2015

SDK never meets a stranger. He talks to everyone who crosses his path. As a recovering Helicopter Mom, I am learning to give him space to establish and nurture relationships independent of me. Well, today we (he) went fishing again. Twin boys and their father joined us on the pier. SDK asked them a series of questions, one after another. Although they didn't appear to be annoyed, I wanted SDK to give them space. Then a quiet voice said to me, "That's the way YOU see the world. Give him space to do his thing." Once again, SDK amazed me with his social skills, and once again I was touched by the kindness of strangers. When SDK noticed that they were catching fish and he wasn't, he walked over and said, "Hey, dude! What are you using for bait?" LOL! Next thing I know, the boys' father changes SDK's hook to a smaller one from his tackle box and he and his sons took turns baiting my baby's hook with Nathan's hot dogs. SDK made two friends and caught three fish!

Today was a good day!

#OurCommunity #ILoveMySuperKid #ItTakesAVillage

August 9, 2015

Earlier this week, SDK asked me to teach him how to be cool. I was like "Whaaaat!? You are cool." He then explained to me that he wanted to be cool and make friends on the playground. "Ooooh, Mommy understands. We just need to practice the rhythm of conversation so you can hold a kid's attention long enough for them to see how cool you already are." So SDK and I practiced the rhythm of conversation. We scripted out what he would say and practiced our rhythm. Today we went to Water Mine and BOOM! My baby did it! "Hey, Kid. What's your name? Wanna play with me?" Yes! Indeed! SDK made a park buddy! WINNING! (If you are interested in seeing our rhythm of conversation practice, check out my FB page. I'll post the video.)

#SocialSkills #Autism #BigKids #ILoveMySuperKid #SoProud

August 12, 2015

When it comes to SDK, I leave nothing to chance. We practice every concept and routine. Then I provide him with visual aids to reinforce. He is going to visit his grandparents, so we practiced FaceTiming, and I sent this visual aid to his iPad to remind him of the process.

#MakeItConcrete

#Practice

#ProvidesAidsForReinforcement

#WatchThemFlourish

#Independence

#BigKidsStuff

#BornToWin

#ILoveMySuperKid

#Autism

#WeGotThis

August 12, 2015

Just when I'm thinking about how much I miss him already, I look up and see shoe tracks on the ceiling of my car. Umm, yeah, I'm good for now… #ThatChild

August, 15, 2015

During our FaceTime conversation, SDK stops talking and is just looking at the screen.
Me: Why are you so quiet?
Ricky II: I'm thinking.
Me: What are you thinking about?
Ricky II: I'm just thinking that you are so pretty.
#MyBaby
#ILoveMySuperKid
#CountdownTilHeComesHome

September 3, 2015

There is a trailer floating around the Internet for a comic book about a little boy with super powers and his widowed mom. Several of my friends have either tagged me on posts about it or sent me the trailer because the trailer reminds them of Ricky II and me. What an absolute blessing that so many people see my child and connect him to a story of a mom raising a super hero.

Some years ago I met Johnny Earle, Founder of Johnny Cupcakes, and I told him I had a son on the autism spectrum. His immediate response was, "Autism! That's his super power!"

At that time, Super Kid was a private name I called Ricky II. I labeled his backpack with "Super Kid," and the kindergarten teacher communication journal I sent him to school with daily was called the Super Kid Book because anything Ricky II needed help with in school I asked his teacher to write it in the book in the form of a positive message. I would read Ricky II's Super Kid Book daily, and we would work on whatever was listed for that day. Whether it was learning to pull the sleeves of his jacket right side out after taking his jacket off in the morning so he could quickly get it on and get in line for recess without additional assistance, or putting a straw through a juice box by himself, or sitting criss-cross applesauce, or how to raise his hand to get the teacher's attention, or how to walk in line with his hand by his side, or how to use an inside voice, and a myriad of other things that many kids would generally learn intuitively, Ricky II and I would practice each day in our home.

I've always told Ricky II we would practice things so much because we were building up his super powers. So when I met Johnny and he said "super power," I was moved to tears because he saw the world the way I saw the world. In that moment, I realized if he could see autism as a super power, and I saw autism as a super power, then others could see autism as a super power. And I started publicly calling Ricky II Super Kid. Soon others started referring to Ricky II through the lens by which I saw my son. I never saw autism as debilitating. My son's beautiful brain worked differently, and it was my job, as mom, to step into his world, figure it out, and teach him from that prospective with each lesson and strategy I developed for and taught to Ricky II. I am helping my baby hone his super powers.

Now when people talk to me, even people I am meeting for the first time, they ask me, "How is Super Kid?" And each time I hear someone say "Super Kid," my heart explodes with pride. As of late, I have had parents or friends of parents reach out to me and say, "I have a Super Kid" or "My friend has two Super Kids." The world and its perspective of diverse learners is slowly changing, and I am so grateful that God gave me a small role to play in that forward movement.

Our Super Kids work so hard every day to do simple tasks that many take for granted. But they keep trying and trying until they get it! And once they get it, they got it! BOOM! A new super power! Then we are on to hone the next super power. Sometimes I think it must be exhausting to be Ricky II. I've never had to work as hard as he does daily for anything. But he lives life with a song in his heart and a genuine smile on his face. He is my greatest teacher.

Thank you, Village, for recognizing my baby as a Super Kid. I ask that you join me in celebrating and carving out a space in our hearts and world for all the Super Kids who work so hard every day honing their super powers. BOOM! POW! BANG! BAM!
#ILoveOurSuperKids
#TheyGotThis

September 5, 2015

I stand in constant amazement of SDK... He is a "Seize the Moment" child. Today when we were leaving the Sprayground, the attendant was giving the 15 minutes to closing call on the megaphone. Fascinated by the loud sound... SDK walked over to the attendant...

SDK: Hey, what's that?

Guy: A megaphone.

SDK: What did you say?

Guy: I told everyone we will be closing in 15 minutes.

SDK: Oh, can I tell everybody?

Guy: No... it's for us to use... (He turns to go in the building then he turns back around) Sure, Why not!

SDK: *a million-watt smile* *chest pumped*

That young man made My Child's day!!

While walking to the car....

SDK: You know why he let me do that? Because I'm Super! #ThatsAFactJack
#BOOM
#ILoveMySuperKid

September 8, 2015

First Day of 3rd Grade!!! READY!!!!

September 8, 2015

He is just TOO COOL for SCHOOL!!! Get 'em,
SuperDuperKid!!!!!!! BOOM!!!!
#ILoveMySuperKid
#TeamSDK

MAMA BEAR'S BIG BOY
NINE YEARS OLD

September 20, 2015

SDK is my greatest teacher. Even on his birthday, he gave me the gift of a beautiful and powerful lesson. I love parties. I like to plan them. I like to attend them, and I have always made a very big deal of SDK's birthday parties. SDK's parties have always been very well attended. But the families present were generally an extension of SDK's parents' relationships. I always kept a pretty hearty group of mommy friends so birthday parties were a yearly rotation of my friends and their kids. Well, last year there was a shift…

As children get older, relationships become more cerebral and parents can no longer put them in a pen like puppies and just say "Play." Relationships begin to develop based on common interests. SDK's unilateral interests coupled with his emerging social skills result in being the odd man out at times. SDK doesn't notice, but I do.

Last month, I asked SDK what did he want to do for his birthday. He told me he wanted to go to Build-A-Bear and PF Chang with J_ and L_. My first thought was, "That's not a party. That's a play date." But he was adamant about spending his birthday with only these two children. I followed his wishes. We called Build-A-Bear and were told we needed at least five children to reserve a party. I turned to SDK. He said, "Nope, I just want J_ and L_ for my party."

The day of his party arrives and I'm a little nervous because I've never attended a birthday party with only two guests. If one doesn't show up, that's half his guest list. Well, they both showed up, and I can say without question that I just attended the best birthday party I've ever been blessed to witness. The day was so intentional and truly a celebration of My Child. He was with people who not only liked him but understood him, had a relationship with him, and loved him for exactly who he is. When he opened his gifts from them, I could tell they knew My Child. Those were SDK's favorite things! These two children really knew my baby. They were his FRIENDS.

I am so proud that my 9 year old was able to choose quality over quantity. Today, I heard him laugh from his belly with his head thrown back as his friends got his quirky sense of humor. He was completely in his element. Last year, SDK received two birthday party invitations from classmates... J_ and L_. I guess he noticed more than I gave him credit for...

Do YOU, SDK! You teach your mama a new lesson every day.

❤ ❤ ❤ ❤ #ILoveMySuperKid #HappyBirthday #MyChild

CLOSING

RICKY II HAS celebrated his ninth birthday, which signifies the end of early childhood. I know in my heart that I have equipped him with the tools he needs to be successful in all areas of his young life.

All of the lessons I learned as a young woman gave me the knowledge I needed to work with my son as his first teacher and greatest advocate. All of the hardship I experienced as a child motivated me to protect him with all I have in me. I have watched with pride and astonishment as he has grown and developed into a happy, confident, and brilliant little person. Now I have to trust the process, the process of growth. I planted the seed when he was an infant in my arms. I pressed his seed deep into the rich and cultivated soil—the life experiences that prepared me to be his mother. I watered the soil daily by learning more skills so I could better assist in his growth and development. I added fertilizer by seeking out help to enrich him in areas where I was not as strong so his growth could be further assisted. I was a greenhouse protecting him from the elements of harm and providing him a safe place to grow. I was the sunshine shining on him positive affirmation so he would have the light he needed to grow strong roots. Although I could not see the transformation of his seed beneath the soil, I trusted God and the germination process. I could not see the seed open up and develop roots, but I trusted the process and continued to garden. Then from the soil a strong seedling appeared, and I had physical evidence that the work I had done was not in vain. I have watched that seedling develop and sprout beautiful bright green and uniquely shaped leaves. I have given him roots so deep that I know he has a strong foundation and is now able to support the growth of whatever fruit God has purposed him to bear. I am so excited to see the super fruit that is going to come from Ricky II's tree.

Although I wish I could hold him in my arms forever and keep him close to me and under my watchful eye, I know it is time for me to take a step back and give him room to spread his branches and bear his fruit. But I will cover him every morning as he heads to school with a very special prayer.

The Mama Bear Prayer

Dear Father,

*Thank You so much for entrusting me to guide this little soul
to greatness.*

*Please let the words from my mouth uplift and nurture
his spirit.*

*Let the love in my heart cover him completely, when I am near
and when I am far.*

Protect him always.

Place people in his path with good hearts and helping hands.

I know through You all things are possible.

*Open his mind to receive the information being taught to him
for his betterment, and*

Keep his heart open so good people are drawn to him.

Lord, give me the strength to trust and let go when needed, and

*Give me the discernment to know when to speak up for his
emotional, physical, and intellectual needs.*

And give me the courage to do so quickly and with confidence.

*I know he belongs to You and thank You every day for choosing
me to be his mother on Earth. Be with us always.*

Amen